Witchcraft and Occult

A Basic Guide for Modern Witches to Find Their Own Path

(A Beginner's Journey Compendium of Spells, Rituals and Occult Knowledge)

Warren Garner

Published By **Jordan Levy**

Warren Garner

All Rights Reserved

Witchcraft and Occult: A Basic Guide for Modern Witches to Find Their Own Path (A Beginner's Journey Compendium of Spells, Rituals and Occult Knowledge)

ISBN 978-1-7752436-1-8

No part of this guidebook shall be reproduced in any form without permission in writing from the publisher except in the case of brief quotations embodied in critical articles or reviews.

Legal & Disclaimer

The information contained in this book is not designed to replace or take the place of any form of medicine or professional medical advice. The information in this book has been provided for educational & entertainment purposes only.

The information contained in this book has been compiled from sources deemed reliable, and it is accurate to the best of the Author's knowledge; however, the Author cannot guarantee its accuracy and validity and cannot be held liable for any errors or omissions. Changes are periodically made to this book. You must consult your doctor or get professional medical advice before using any of the suggested remedies, techniques, or information in this book.

Upon using the information contained in this book, you agree to hold harmless the Author from and against any damages, costs, and expenses, including any legal fees potentially resulting from the application of any of the information provided by this guide. This disclaimer applies to any damages or injury caused by the use and application, whether directly or indirectly, of any advice or information presented, whether for breach of contract, tort, negligence, personal injury, criminal intent, or under any other cause of action.

You agree to accept all risks of using the information presented inside this book. You need to consult a professional medical practitioner in order to ensure you are both able and healthy enough to participate in this program.

Table Of Contents

Chapter 1: What Is Wicca? 1

Chapter 2: Law Of Threefold 9

Chapter 3: Perfect Time For Doing Magick 20

Chapter 4: What Is Magick? 39

Chapter 5: Simple Paper Magick 69

Chapter 6: Divination Tools Used In Wicca 76

Chapter 7: Walking The Path Of Wicca And Being A Witch 85

Chapter 8: What Does Witch Mean? 89

Chapter 9: Witchcraft And Religion 115

Chapter 10: Great Witch, Bad Witch: Which Is Which? 147

Chapter 11: Detecting Energy Currents 173

Chapter 1: What Is Wicca?

Wicca is a thriving 20th-century cult of contemporary witchcraft which assists its adherents to connect more deeply with Nature as well as Mother Earth. With its teachings, the faith of Wicca is a way to increase awareness, love and reverence towards Nature, Sun and the sun moon, rivers, wind mountain ranges, rain the animal kingdom, flowering plants and plants, as well as the earth beneath our feet, and the beautiful autumn colors and winter snow.

Wicca is a way of understanding that everything we see is comprised from energy. It is a belief in the dual nature throughout all of creation. This implies the existence of an God and Goddess, feminine and masculine energy both positive and negative. The entire Universe is composed of this energies and Nature is itself a stunning illustration of the duality principle humans have the potential of duality within us.

In Wicca The Gods and Goddesses exist present within us and in us. They are depicted as gentle and gentle beings The gods aren't violent toward their children. They don't hold grudges, they do not are not averse to punishment and don't create Heaven or Hell. They are instead compassionate, understanding and encourage respect and fairness.

Wicca is a way to take complete responsibility for the actions we take and doesn't support any behaviour or claims made by the outside world, such as the Devil who manipulates us to do things that are not good.

This is where the idea of Karma is a part of the notion that what you do in the world is returned to you as people, energy, as well as situations. Wiccans are not believers the existence of Satan as well as any other symbol of Evil. These concepts are typically found in Christian beliefs. There is also no assertion of particularity regarding this being the only way to peace, understanding or wisdom. However, the principles of Wicca allow the person to discover and select the path that best suits them through the world. This philosophy reflects the idea of Nature is sacred, and Life is worthy of respect, regardless of the way in the medium through which it manifests.

The History of Wicca and Witchcraft

The word Wicca is derived from the Anglo - Saxon word "wicce" that means wisdom. Wicca as a religion is an expression from Neo - Pagan Witchcraft. Both terms are in a lot of ways similar but they have several significant distinctions. It is possible to be Wiccan without practicing witchcraft, and one can be a Wiccan but not practice witchcraft, and you can also be a witch and also practice Witchcraft while not following the rules of Wicca.

The story of Wicca and Witchcraft is awash with myths of half-truths, prejudices, and misunderstandings which a majority of them began around the middle age. Many of us have heard and have read about how the Inquisition was used to hunt down and adduce, torture and even kill those suspected of practicing witchcraft.

The practice of witchcraft began at the time of the first civilizations that humans have ever lived in. The term witchcraft is also referred to by the name of "The Craft of the Wise." Witches can be male or female, and they each believed in their own Spirit of Nature. They had a wealth in knowledge about plants, medicine as well as food, and their life was heavily centered around creating the connection to Mother Earth.

Discoveries in archeology have revealed 40.000 years of evidence from Paleolithic people who worshipped an Hunter God as well as an fertility goddess. Wicca emphasizes the spiritual and peaceful side of Nature that nurtures and provides you with the opportunity to live. Witches are also intermediaries between the physical world as well as the spiritual.

Gerald Gardner was a British civil servant, who claimed the Wicca Coven he was in joined Wicca Coven in 1939. In 1949, he the author wrote a work on Wicca "High Magick's Aid". In the words of Gardner, Wicca is a faith that is a combination of the Goddess as well as a Horned God that is part of The Ancient North European Pagan Beliefs. However, regardless of these claims nevertheless, we are aware that Wicca is a contemporary version of a religion that has its origins as far back as the earliest human civilizations.

Wicca Goddess and Gods

The faith of Wicca depicts Nature as being created and governed by two primary factors: The masculine God and the Goddess of feminine form. The Goddess and God are the makers of every both physical and spiritual realities, in both visible and unobserved existence. Together, they bring peace to all living things and neither can exist in isolation from the other.

In Nature We all carry the energy of both in our bodies. The practitioners of Wicca don't wait until certain dates or events to do a ceremony for the purpose of connecting to the divine. God as well as Goddess.

In particular, keeping a close eye of the natural beauty which surrounds you, vegetation, the mountains as well as animals, and taking in your surroundings, watching the Sun as it sets and rises, as well as the Moon are considered as ceremonies in them. Wiccans acknowledge the existence of God as well as Goddess all around us.

In the world of Wicca the gods and goddesses are given a variety of names. Some are known as Nameless.

It is likely that you've heard certain Goddesses with names such as Aphrodite, Diana, Freya, Gaia, Inanna and Nut/Nuit. Some of the most frequently-used God names include Pan, Eros, Apollo, Horus, Osiris, Ra and Thorus. It is likely that you recognize some names that were mentioned as in the sense that they are similar to names that are used in Greek as well as Egyptian theology and culture. Wicca believers see Goddesses and Gods in any or all of the forms they feel at ease with. The Divine can be found everywhere. They look at the Sun and praise their God for all the good fortune they've received in the planet.

In Wicca the Goddess is represented by the Three Goddesses

It is an emblem of the three phases of life.

As Maiden, symbolized by the changing moon - symbolizes young, innocent and tender young girl

Mother, symbolized with the full moon, represents motherhood, mature protection and caring woman at her motherhood phase.

The Crone symbol represents the waning moon as a sign of the elderly woman knowledgeable and a great teacher of wisdom.

Chapter 2: Law Of Threefold

"Bide to the Wiccan Law ye must

Perfect love and total faith

Eight words that the Wiccan Reed will

Do no harm to anyone Do what you want to"

- Unknown

The Wiccan Rede symbolizes the ethical rules of people who adhere to the Wicca route. It represents the Wicca version of the Law of Cause and Effect'.

The phrase "Rede" originates from the older English phrase "roedan" which means to control, or to guide. This is the Wiccan Law of three was first written at the start of the 20th century. It was written by unidentified sources.

Wicca is a belief system that teaches us to emit energy into the Universe by our actions and words, and that whatever energy we put out, we receive it back in three levels. Wiccans are adamant about the freedom to exercise their will and energy at will as they do not endanger any other person. They believe that the Law of Three has directs the emotional, physical and spiritual life of the followers. Wiccans are of the belief that in the end each person is responsible for the choices and actions. Finding ways to influence other people or achieving your goals with the help of others is forbidden within Wicca. Wiccans do not practice worship or are they believers in Satan or human sacrifices. They do not belong to this religious belief. People who use black magic to influence others, or attempt to hurt others aren't thought of as Wiccan.

Sabbats

There are Sabbats and Esbats actually occur that occur in Nature. Sabbats follow the solar calendar, and honor the celebration of God and the Sun as the masculine energy of The All. Sabbats are the natural cycles of Earth. They are between eight and ten Sabbats, and they are the equinoxes, those two days during the year that daylight and night are equal in duration. being the longest as well as the shorter day of the calendar as well as the longest night of the year, also known as the solstice. They are the middle point between these natural phenomena.

The Sabbats are the middle points between these four events are the peak of each of the seasons. They are also known as the Sabbats of Majority.

Samhain: October 31

It is also known as Halloween, or the New Year of the Witch. This is among the major holidays of Wicca as it is an important spiritual celebration. The day of this celebration is dedicated to those who have died, since they commemorate the passing of the Lord. According to some, during this time, the line between living people and dead is at its thinnest. On this day, people offer food for the loved ones who passed away.

Yule: December 21 Winter solstice

The lengthiest night during the entire year. It is the time when God returns to life and light returns to Earth. The celebrations celebrate this with gifts exchanged as an indication of a better tomorrow.

Imbolc: February 2

It is also known as Brigid's day-keeper of the holy fire. Imbolc signifies the height of winter and is celebrated by lighting fires as well as candles.

Ostara: March 21

It symbolizes the start of spring and new life. It also symbolizes fertility. It holds the significance for the renewal of Nature and is believed to be the period for new ideas as well as personal growth. Wiccans are celebrating this by eating boiled eggs, and prayers to a brighter future.

Beltane: May 1st

It is the time of peak spring and is celebrated as a day that God and Goddess join in a holy union. Beltane is a celebration of the renewal of life as well as the greenness of nature and blooming flowers and trees. It's a perfect time for flowers being delivered to your house.

Summer Solstice: June 21: A midsummer

It is the beginning of summer is the longest day in the entire year. It is an ideal time for healing spells, particularly through ceremonies outdoors. In this season, nature is at its best.

Lughnassad 2. August the first harvest

It marks the beginning of the harvest season, Lughnassad is also referred to for being the Feast of Bread and is typically the time to bake bread. When performing ceremonies, Wiccans decorate their altar by putting up fruits and other vegetables.

Mabon: Harvest 21st, September festival

The duration of evening and day are identical and marks the beginning to darkness and winter. In this period, Wiccans celebrate and give gratitude for God for the bounty they of the year.

Esbats

Esbats are Moon ceremonies that help Wicca is a celebration of Goddesses and feminine energies. Esbats ceremonies usually honor the full moon, and it is believed that at full moon, the goddess's powers are the most powerful.

Each month at least one time Wiccans and Witches pay homage to the Goddess with a celebration of any of the three moon phases, according to the type of energy they require for them.

- New Moon

Wiccans practice rituals during the New Moons when they require the beginning of anew chapter, to start afresh within their lives.

- The Waxing Moon

It is that season when the illuminated portion of the moon gets in size and brightness. This is regarded as the best opportunity to experience more positive energy and energy in the pursuit of all new targets you've set during the full moon.

-The Full Moon

This is when the moon's energies are at their maximum. This is the best time to use your magic and pursue your desires. The three days preceding and following that Full Moon are considered a period of tremendous impact and power as is when the moon is full. moon.

-The Waning Moon

It is the time of year in which the moon gets smaller. It is also the ideal opportunity to rid yourself of everything negative that you have. It can manifest itself in many forms but it's crucial to remember that nobody should be hurt in the procedure.

A solar year is comprised of 13 full moons. 29.5-day moon cycle 1 each year is characterized by one full moon each month and one additional moon named Blue Moon. Blue Moon.

January: Wolf Moon

Now is the perfect time for self-evaluation. Consider yourself the seed you have placed in the ground, and is eagerly waiting to rebirth.

February: Storm Moon

The perfect time to clear rid of negative thoughts. The full moon symbolizes self-forgiveness as well as mental home cleaning as well as self-purification.

March: Chaste Moon

It's a great time to make new startings and for you to get started on those projects you set out to complete this fall, and to set the goals to develop.

April: Seed Moon

This is the time to celebrate fertility, wisdom and expansion. The perfect moment to see the beginnings of your magical abilities. You can now move from thinking to doing.

May: Hare Moon

Celebration of the joys of life, health, and truly loving relationships. A great time to be yourself as you truly are and to spend the time to live your love affair.

June: Dryad Moon

The moon is also known in the world of Strawberry Moon, it represents the full moon of love that provides energy to the marriage, love and happiness. An opportunity to care for your garden.

July: Mead Moon

It is a great time to contemplate to dream work, prosperity and meditation. Magick is a powerful experience during this time of the year can be a truly amazing experience.

August: Wyrt Moon

It's the perfect time to reap advantages of your work, and to thank God as well as the Goddess for the bounty attained, your craft skills and the determination.

September: Harvest Moon

The time for prosperity and protection. The perfect time to organize your mental and spiritual health following the heat of summer.

October: Blood Moon

Make use of the lunar energies to assist in creating new goals, enhancing your spirituality, reflect on rebirth, death, and consider the possibility of reincarnation.

Chapter 3: Perfect Time For Doing Magick

If we consider magick, the picture that appears we see typically involves doing nighttime rituals. As I said earlier, Wiccan God is represented through the Sun and the Sunlight. It is possible to conduct an ritual whenever you feel it is the right time for you, regardless of whether it's in the morning or in the evening.

Magical rituals at dawn

Dawn itself is a magical moment in the daytime and a time where dawn is slowly rising up, and the sky is half-light and half-dark. This is the ideal moment to think about the creation of new thoughts, beginnings and spiritual awakening. Witches in the past took advantage of the dawn hours to create love potion.

Sunrise magick ritual

The world is awakening. The Sun is rising and the light of it is getting more intense.

As you get up early in the morning don't forget to recollect your dreams and meditate at least 5 minutes in order to recharge your energy. It is the perfect moment to make spells that will help you achieve your goals as well as to get rid of the negative behaviors. Cast spells to end smoking cigarettes or shed weight. Set your oracle or tarot cards on the table and imagine the next day.

Magical rituals during Noon

The energy of God has reached its highest and is at its most intense in this time. It is a huge amount of energy available for your magical abilities. Utilize this energy to build the strength you need and tackle things you believe you're struggling to conquer

Magick rituals during Dusk

The day's light is fading and the dark night is beginning to creep up. It is the time of year that the doors of the realm of magic are to be opened, and performing magical ceremonies during this time can give you access to these realms. The connection with divine energies is particularly strong.

Magick nighttime ritual

The power of the Goddess is very powerful at late at night. It is now time to think about the past day and focus on good experiences. Use this positive energy to cast spells and bring more good things into your life.

Midnight ritual of magick

The term "Witch Hour" is also used to describe Witch Hour represents the perfect moment to commune to Goddess and soak up the spirituality associated with the Moon. It is the perfect opportunity to connect with the wisdom of your heart and personal world. Do a ritual, and then use a spell to eliminate all negativity as well as to tap into healing energies from the Universe. Make a fire in the honour of the goddess and remain silent. Then you will be able to hear her words of wisdom. Request her guidance and support, ask for her help in your daily life, and then as the sun shines brightly, you can you can ask her to illuminate your way. It is at this point that you are able to feel the force of her love.

Stones and Crystals in Magick

The entire universe of healing stones, crystals, semi-precious stones is composed of a powerful source of energy within the Earth's center. The term gemstone is associated with strength and power along with wealth and desire as well as nature and magick. They are used for a myriad of reasons such as healing and meditation in order to replenish your energy with positive vibrations as well as gaining insight and dedication. They are also utilized for talismans and amulets since they are infused with their own energy and frequency of vibration.

In rituals of magick, they can be used as amulets for healing purposes and for gaining energy.

In the course of a ritual place the gemstone you prefer with you then close your eyes. pay attention to its energy. See how it flows throughout your body.

Each stone serves a purpose in relation to magical rituals:

Sapphire, as a gem occurs in a deep blue hue however it may be found in yellow black, green and gray.

Blue sapphire has a connection to the solar system Saturn. It symbolizes of wisdom, aristocracy and strength and loyalty. The belief is that this stone improves eye sight and longevity.

Additionally, it can be employed to treat depression, clinical and skin issues as well as cancer and insomnia. Additionally, it can help keep you on your spiritual path, and to maintain your the highest levels of focus on yourself. Blue is the color that Sapphire can also help you awaken and activate it's Throat and Third Eye chakras.

Ruby is closely associated with our celestial body that is, the Sun. The color is reddish, and it is a stone that symbolizes nobility and purity. It also brings high energy success and leadership. Ruby boosts our vitality (chi which is also called prana) is a shield against unhappy feelings and aids in decision-making and setting goals. Ruby is also a great way to increase heart power, enhances the function of blood circulation and the circulation system, speeds up elimination, helps protect the embryo kidneys, the embryo, as well as the eyes. It's highly linked with the root chakra, and assists in opening the chakra.

Moonstone just like the moon is a symbol of mystery. As represented by the Moon It is the stone of tranquility spirituality, inner explorations, and fresh startings. Moonstone improves intuition and sensitivity as well as aids in weight loss as well as water retention and hormonal issues. Additionally, it has beneficial effects for those suffering from depression and anxiety. It activates the energy of kundalini and helps bring out the best of individuals. In conjunction with the goddess It connects the energy and the spirits of Nature. It can be worn as a talisman in order to enhance and improve the persona.

The Tiger Eye is connected to Mercury. Mercury. The stone is regarded as the stone that brings luck, fortune, and security. It assists in the regenerating of energy in the body; it rejuvenates cells and helps reduce frequent convulsions, pains and body toxicity. Also, it can be beneficial on treating throat issues and anemia. Tiger eye is well-known for its spiritual benefits and assists to connect and communicate with your child within and protects you from the bad spirits. Aids in bringing forth prosperity and wealth on the physical level and can also have positive impact on the Root as well as the Solar Plexus chakras.

There is a long-standing tradition of using amulets made from stones.

To get the best results You can create your own crystal that carries the energy of your own. In the course of the ritual, you should hold the stone in your hands and imagine that it is in charge of your energies and the energy of God as well as Goddess. Write and think about it in order to assign the intention of the stone. The purpose could be the protection of finances, security, and love or whatever else you want to do to do with it.

It is important to remember to wash your stones frequently. It is possible to bury them in the ground for 24 hours or set the stones out under the night light. Whichever option you pick make sure you are aware of the stones you have chosen as they're part of the world around you and contain your energies.

Once you've used them for a specific amount duration, for example several years, think about giving them back to Mother Earth. Put them back in the earth And remember that you can never stop reviving with fresh ideas and energy for your own life as well as the future.

Using Oils in Your Magick

It is very simple to incorporate into your magical routines and everyday rituals. They are able to assist you in attracting the things you desire and require to be successful in your lives. Think about what you wish for or require to be fulfilled in your life. Then, at that point, place a couple of drops of oil on the flame. The drops of oil do not ignite however they are instantly heated and disperse and emit their aromas throughout the air. In doing so it's beneficial to use spells in chanting to boost the effect of the ceremony. Here's an example the spell that you could make use of, or make your own spell, and then use the spell to suit your specific requirements:

The magickal oil is burned

I wish peace to my life come back

The words are to be spelled to you

I will listen to them. Set me free

I wish joy and love to stay within my heart

I'd like to make this my goal, so to make it happen.

It is your right to play the song any number of times as you want. There are a range of oils that you could use for specific purposes, such as Love, concentration, achievement and protection. They can also help with confidence as well as peace, harmony insomnia, headaches, fresh opportunities, development and relationships.

The selection of the oils to use for rituals is determined by the intent of the ceremony. What do you require or would like in your own day-to-day life?

If you are looking to draw cash and wealth, then you should consider using Basil oil. It contains Bergamot Cinnamon, Ginger, Pine and Patchouli.

If you want to bring more sexual attraction and love into your life, then you should utilize Cardamom, Clove, Coriander, Geranium, Ginger, Jasmine, Lavender, Magnolia, Rose or Sandalwood.

In order to increase your psychic ability when you meditate and perform rituals it is possible to use Yarrow, Tuberose, Sandalwood, Sandalwood, Peppermint, Magnolia, Lemon Grass or Jasmine.

In order to improve your well-being, consider using Camphor to help with respiratory ailments, Coriander, Cypress for emotional pain, Eucalyptus, Juniper, Palma Rosa or Rosemary. But it should be remembered that these oils is not a substitute for professional medical care.

To combat insomnia, try Lavender, Chamomile, Ceder or Jasmine. When the oil is slowly burning, the words, it is possible to create your own variation for the same reason:

In the presence of this oil that is burning, I used the oil to cast a spell

to have a relaxing evening and to sleep soundly.

To help you meditate, utilize Magnolia oil Juniper, Yarrow or Myrrh.

In order to reduce the negative influence on your daily life, try using Grapefruit, Lemon, Neroli or Yarrow.

Prior to performing any rituals, you must take a purification bath that cleanses your body both physically and mentally. Place a few drops the essential oils you love in warm water, and take pleasure in the relaxing effects and aromas that your bath will emit.

These essential oils work well to use in rituals, prayers or spells and also for empowering yourself. They have a unique strength and when you incorporate them into the magick of your rituals, you can increase this power.

Herbs and Plants in Your Magick Rituals.

Through the ages, Witches have gained substantial understanding of plants and herbs and their application in the field of the healing process and in magick. In the present, Wiccans and Witches use their knowledge of herbs as well as plants to perform rituals as well as when healing. Magick is the way they remain connected to Nature.

Plants and herbs have numerous uses. ones of the most common are:

- Oils

The Wicca practice and its religion is an even greater belief in the power of oil. In order to make oils from the herb you love or plant, you have to wrap your herbs in cheesecloth before putting it in a container of coconut oil, olive oil as well as almond oil, or another oil you like. You can leave it for up to 30 days outdoors in the sun. And be sure to shake the container every daily. The herb extract that you select will be absorbed in the oil base to provide it with its own natural aroma.

- Sachets

Witches create a sachet through adding herbs to a compact bag that is usually made from silk to wear it as an amulet inside their pockets or beneath the pillows.

- Incense

Incense is created by mixing herbs harvested, dried and then blended with other herbs. Incense serves the purpose of lighting in ceremonies.

Bath salts

Both Witches as well as Wiccans can make the bath salts of their choice by grinding and mixing herbs, in conjunction with Epsom salt, or another salt you like.

The mixture is used prior to going through rituals in order to cleanse their energy and body.

Herbs serve a specific purpose within the rituals and beliefs of Wicca.

Dandelion can be used to call spirits, and for connecting to Divination.

Frankincense is a great way to cleanse negative energies and it can be employed to help connect you to your soul and Spirit World.

Ginseng is wonderful for love, passion, as well as for healing.

Jasmine can be used to bring an abundance of physical and financial wealth in your life. It also promotes sleep, and love.

The use of mustard is to increase fertility as well as improve cognitive performance.

Parsley is a great food for purification and security.

Rose is renowned because of its ability to perform romantic rituals of love.

Violet is a good color to use to protect your spirituality, bring luck and healing.

You may choose to cultivate your own plants and herbs as well as to purchase the herbs from a herbalist. The most crucial step is keep track of allergic reactions that you and your family members might be suffering from in connection with the plants. Be aware that even dried plants may be hazardous for your health if have an allergy to the herbs. Another important aspect is to be aware of which herbs can be poisonous. Avoid coming in the vicinity of these herbs, and should not consume their products through smoking or drinking. The most effective way to avoid them is switch them out with another herb.

Utilize your home-made oils with a candle to achieve the best result from your ritual. Incense is burned while you perform the ritual, and then draw the circle in a clockwise direction to protect yourself. Inhale the incense's smoke to clear your space free of negativity. Also, make sure the windows are shut. When you move from one area to the another, you could consider singing these phrases.

If you are a victim of negative energies, you might never be

Please let me go from them

And send them away.

Alongside cleansing your home of negative vibrations and noise, you should consider installing protective plants around your residence.

Chapter 4: What Is Magick?

Let me first clarify the distinction of "magic" and "magick".

Magic is often associated with illusions, shows as well as stage shows. However, it is also a matter of involves the energy. The word "K" holds a special position in the realm of Wicca and occultism since it's the eleventh letter of the alphabet. its symbolism is the undiscovered and hidden realms.

The main reason to practice magick is tapping into the subconscious mind, and unlock intuition, spirituality and creativity. That is why practicing the art of magick and performing magical rituals assist you in using your mind to be more productive and creative manner.

It's hard to define precisely what magick is since we can't see the whole range of light like UV light and x-rays. That's the situation for the magick. The power of magick is felt but cannot be visible. This is the energy that us from within our being, from Nature, God, Goddess and even the universe.

The main purpose of doing magick through Wicca is to create an association with the divine. The benefits and spiritual purposes that are gained from performing magick are endless. Being a religion of Nature, Wicca teaches us that the real magick exists within every one of us. It is possible to tap into this energy anytime we want to heal our own bodies or world in order to achieve our desires as well as give peace to our souls and peace in our relations. The energy you receive is yours to keep and nobody can prevent you in gaining benefits by it. Make use of it with care and not harm.

Create your personal Book of Shadows.

Through the ages the witches' records have been kept of each spell they have performed, every ritual they've conducted as well as the plant-based remedies and cures such as oils, crystals, oil and every aspect of their knowledge about nature, the Universe, Nature and their ways of living. To protect their way of life, and heritage they utilized their Runic alphabet to put all of their knowledge in books. It is now known as"the "Book of Shadows", "Book of Magick" or "Grimoire", it should be an everyday read for all Wicca person or Witch.

Start your personal Book of Shadows just by recording your ideas, thoughts, opinions as well as ritual thoughts and emotions every day. Record the principles you would like to follow but they should not be in favor of inflicting injury to another person. If you're a member of an order of coven, and you follow the rules of a particular group and you want to create a piece of writing about the guidelines. Also, you can write the shorter or longer variant of the Wiccan Rede if you like.

Create a piece of writing about God and Goddess and how you feel about them. Also, write about how you see them as well as what they represent to you. Write about your feelings the first time you made the decision to devote the rest of your time to Wicca. Create the Book of Shadows more practical by keeping track of the different phases in rituals like the Moon, Sabbats, and Esbats ceremonies. It is possible to write about the crystals you love and what you find you connecting with them as well as with herbs, oils and candles. You might want to write about subjects that are more personal to you including your own rituals, and the transformations that you've experienced over some time of practicing these rituals.

Note down your wishes and rituals. Make a note of the symbols and dreams you have since this is the method by which God and Goddess communicate with you.

It's your private Book of Shadows so feel at ease to be yourself. Make sure to keep it a secret, and only share your secrets with people who are like you or not any at all, if it feels more at ease for you. The Book of Shadows will be the most precious asset you have as well as a way to increase personal growth and awareness as a an integral part of Wicca tradition.

Basic Magic Tools for Beginner

If you think Wicca is the right choice for you and want to begin practicing the art of Wicca, it isn't necessary to go broke to buy these items or via the Internet.

Start by buying items and things that you can purchase for lesser money.

Begin with candles since they're not expensive and come in a variety of dimensions, shapes and colors. Candle holders can be bought easily. Also, you can try your hand at making one yourself. an attempt at creating an individual one.

Crystals and stones are utilized in the art of the art of magick. It is not necessary to purchase a lot of crystals in one go. Begin with a handful to discover how you can connect to these. You can find them everywhere and the collection is sure to expand as time passes.

- Divination tools: tarot cards, oracles, runes etc. They can be used to make the right choices, developing your psychic skills and getting the needed solutions.

Feathers are required however, you don't require them to purchase, because you can discover them. The feather symbolizes the element Air.

Holy water can be utilized to cleanse your magic items

The pentacle is utilized as a pendant or you could place it on an altar to provide security. Noting that the four five pentagram points symbolize the elements: Earth Air, Water, and Water. The fifth symbolises the Spirit.

Salt represents the salt of the Earth as well as employed to create holy water to aid in magical purposes.

Incense is available as a cone, stick or powder. It represents the element Air. In addition, it is used as a component in Air Magick.

The use of music is in rituals. It's a powerful way to increase your own energy level and can also be used to relax the mind as well as the soul. It is possible to play music during a ceremony or dancing to your most sacred music.

The wand can be used for directing energies during rituals. They can be created out of various substances.

Magick Circle and Sacred Altar

If you're just beginning to learn about Wicca or Witchcraft and want to carry out a ritual of magick one of the first things you should be able to master is casting an esoteric circle. This is, thankfully, the easiest to master and is the one that's most vital. The good news is that it's straightforward and it is still among the most crucial aspect of the rituals. The act of casting a circle protects your body from destructive, negative forces.

Pick a quiet spot to enjoy your time, either outdoors or indoors, and pick the best time for your ritual that you are certain you will not be at risk of being disturbed.

Clear the area with vigor by using your wand or the broom to eliminate negative energy from the area. Incense can also be used to achieve this goal.

Crystals can be used for defining your circle. Or sprinkle salt. Also, you can create a circle using your athame, or perhaps you could use candles to create circles with candles. If you choose to conduct your ceremony outdoors it is possible to use rocks or even branches to serve the same intention. When you cast your circle you must walk in a steady pace, think of a large circle of positive energy surrounding you. You can also imagine the circle you cast as a magick web growing around you.

Be aware that your circle, once made, is not removed until the ceremony is carried out. This is the reason you must carry everything that you require in the circle. If, for any reason, you need to leave the circle, you can use your athame to draw a magical entrance. Never break the whole circle. The Altar is considered to be a sacred place in which you honor your God and Goddess. Cast an oath, meditate, make offerings, and so on.

After everything has been prepared Set your altar to face toward the north.

The God objects should be put on the right, while the Goddess items should be placed on the left.

They are the things which you'll most likely use during your daily rituals.

Two candles represent God and God and Goddess

one God statue and a Goddess statue

A table for offering

A glass of wine for an offer

- - Caution and spell materials

- Water bowl: which represents the element water

A lighter that represents the South

A bell used to signal the elements, and break up the circle

- Incense

Feather to symbolize the Air

A bowl of salt is used in order to symbolize the earth

- Pentacle

Casting an imaginary circle

Four candles represent the four elements. But should you not have room at your altar, you may use candles without.

When you have cast your magical circle and place your altar (without lighting candles) you are now ready to call upon your Elements that comprise the Earth as well as God as well as Goddess to be part of your circle.

Be sure to treat your guardians with respect since they're there to keep watch over your activities and you. They'll assist with the magick of your work if you need it.

Turn your face North and summon the spirit of North. These are some suggestions for invocations but you are able to make your own invocation if you prefer:

"Guardians of North," components of Earth

I invite you to be part of my ritual in complete harmony, love and peace'

The candle represents north (use the green candle) Turn clockwise and look east:

"Guardians of East," elements of Air

I would like to invite you to participate in my ritual and keep an eye on me'

Use a yellow candle to light that represents the Air and then face south.

"Guardians of the South elements of sacred Fire

I ask you to be part of this sacred rite'

Use a yellow candle to light that represents the Air to face the south.

"Guardians of the South elements of sacred Fire

I ask you to be part of this sacred rite'

Lighting a candle in red symbolizing the Fire and then face west.

"Guardians of West and elements of water flowing

I ask all of you to participate in this sacred rite'

Lighting an emerald candle, then face toward the north to invoke God or Goddess.

It is also possible to make your own prayers using the words of your choice; it is entirely up to you. Honor God as well as Goddess by burning their candles prior to using them in your prayers.

"Beautiful Lady" goddess of Night

The Queen of All the Wisdom

I will seek you out to find you in Nature as well as in my dreams and magick

Thank you for the moon's light beams

Bring me your mystic illumination

as well as be present during my ritual

I hereby bid you a warm say 'welcome'

'O Great Horned God

I'm contacting you because I'm looking for your assistance.

I will not lie to you. Lord of the earth

Find your strength and independence

You are the Lord of oak and thunder

It is the Lard of the Land as well as hunter

Show me your love

and brings joy from above

I appeal to your light

Take part in my fun

I would like to congratulate you and'welcome'

Once you've completed your ritual, you will not want to cut the circle, and then leave it to the side. After you've invoked the blessings of gods and elements pay respect to them and then thank them for being there. Let them know that you are releasing the deities and elements, they're at peace. Make the circle closed counterclockwise. declare 'Let the circle remain always open, but never broken'.

Thanks to God and goddess for the presence of their gods, and their candles wherever they are. Don't blow out your candles. Instead, just extinguish the flame with the finger tips.

Spellcraft

It's the most innovative aspect of the religion of Wicca casting spells. The spell is a magickal technique that Witches as well as Wiccans utilize to effect modifications to their lives. The term "spell" means 'story' or "fable" to Old English.

It is recommended to make yourself spells. While it might take some time however, it's important because only you can determine what you are missing in your own life. Only you will be able to clearly convey your personal message to God as well as Goddess.

As time passes casting spells will get more effortless. The spells will begin to show changes as you begin doing it regularly, and you become more with Wiccan festivals moon phases, herbal remedies oil, crystals, and other oils.

Consider casting spells only if you are unable to find another way to achieve your goals. It is only when you've exhausted every other option and there is nothing that works. The use of spells is a last resort.

For making the ritual more successful and to increase your chance of success, think about using meditation, creativity as well as the magical tools you use in your ritual.

The concept of imagining is one of magic in and of itself. The imagination is the source of thought, whereas thoughts create our world. Consider long and deeply the goals you wish to reach Create vivid, precise pictures of your goals for the future. Imagine is a influential language in the subconscious. In this case, you need to have faith and trust that the things you think about will be to pass, and that you're capable of achieving such lofty ambitions and successes. If not, it's just an exercise in mental clarity.

The practice of meditation helps you reconnect with your higher self and opens you up to the realm of spirituality as well as higher vibrational entities. Through meditation, you will be able to better feel that you are in the company of God as well as Goddess.

While you study and get more familiar with Wicca and Witchcraft it will become apparent that some spells contain rhymes but that's not the norm. In the case of making your own chants it is your choice to include rhymes when they seem to come natural to you. If they don't bother you, don't be agitated. The trick is to get it done with the help of them. One of the most crucial aspects to do in Spellcraft is to translate the most intense, authentic enthusiasm, passion and energy pictures into words to the best explain what you want the most in that moment.

It is essential to develop a habit of continually striving to improve your self-esteem. Life's basic necessities include cover protection, shelter physical and emotional connection, love and food.

Start small to see if your magick actually works.

Take note that if you're caught in a difficult spot Don't immediately turn to using spells to resolve the issue. Try to look at the issue by a different perspective. Perhaps there's a lesson to learn or even something that is better is just across the street.

When you've finished writing your spell review your intention, and then ask yourself questions to ensure you're on the correct path. Are you getting what you desire?

Do you risk harming someone else when you act that way?

Check the result of your spell since the outcome of your spell will impact

your life. Make sure that your actions do cause harm to someone another's life.

Now, you've double looked over your intentions and how they might affect others. you've gathered the necessary items and your room is ready with an altar and you have cleansed your body energetically. Pick up the piece of paper where the spell was written and into your magical circle, and begin the ritual.

Be aware that you must make a magick circle even if you decide not to go through the whole ritual.

You have realized by today, you're not on your own when it comes to Wicca. The same is true to performing spells or doing magical work. It is possible to call on all the forces of nature, God or Goddess, angels, other gods spirit, and many more.

Entities from various worlds.

It is essential to make use of the strength of one or more components. Based on the element you want to summon it is possible to create an invocation to serve that specific reason.

Before you start, decide which magick you'd like to use. If you're looking to find affection or love, you could be able to invoke elements of Fire and use candles to cast magic. If you want to have more security in your life, then you may want to consider working with using the Earth element, and so on.

Once everything is completed, and you're in a position to invoke the God and Goddess, call the elements into the circle. Light candles as they go and then sit in silence for a few minutes.

Do an hour of meditation in order to be connected to Divinity and then you are able to read aloud your mantra or chant, perform it, whatever you feel most comfortable doing.

When you chant your spell Try to feel the power emanating from your mouth the words you speak, your heart, and the spell you are casting.

You should read it through until you be able to feel the energy around the magical circle. Once you've finished think about your desired outcomes as vividly as you can. Also, you can talk to God, Goddess and the elements of the universe about what you would like to see during this ceremony.

Remember that when you perform an act of worship, you're taken to another dimension that deal with the energies and entities that belong to this realm.

It is merely a tourist there.

Spend some time and be grateful to God as well as Goddess and the elements for being present within your circle.

As long as your memory remains new, write down your experience and write it down within the Book of Shadow.

Be aware that you should never perform a spell on anyone else without permission regardless of how good-hearted you might be. By using rituals and spells you could alter someone's life fate, destiny and free will.

Take note that you should not take money to perform magickal activities since it can degrade the spiritual side of you. If someone is insistent on offering you money, think about donating it to a charitable organization.

Wicca and Witchcraft are based on spirituality Not about materialistic pursuits.

Candle Magick

Candle magick is among the simplest magical arts but it's also among the most effective.

Candle magick can be associated to the element Fire. A thing you must be aware of prior to performing candles magic is Fire is an extremely powerful element that can prove to be extremely damaging if misused. Be sure to reevaluate your motives before performing spells with Fire.

There's no reason to worry about the dimensions, shape and design of your candle. Candles that are used in the home will suffice for their job. There was a time when the people were given a limited selection of choice in regards to candles. Yet they were effective.

Check that the candles are not in use, since the energy accumulated from earlier use could affect the results of the spell adversely. Color is an aspect you should pay attention to since every hue has its own significance and function.

White candles can be utilized for almost any magical spells, however most commonly they are used to enhance meditation, cleaning the house in truth, and for charging positive energy.

Candles in red are used to bring the love of your life into your home as well as a healthy lifestyle and sexual.

The use of green candles is for the purpose of attracting luck and money.

Candles in pink are used to ward off to dispel negativity and divide.

Candles of the color purple are utilized to boost business performance, personal objectives and psychic skills.

It is possible to make your ritual of candle-lighting a straightforward one or opt make it a more complicated ritual. It's dependent on you. one thing you should remember is that the effort that you put into your magick ritual is the main factor.

When you've got the appropriate color candles, you can rub them gently with the oils of your choice and then consider the result you would like to see.

When you are done with the ritual, relax and reflect on your goals, then ignite the candle, and then go through the spell, or make your own mantra.

"I'm now ready to receiving the Divine blessings'

"Money flows more and easier for me'

"May this candle transmit my words in the direction of the Universe and help me to fulfill my

desire into reality.'

Remember the Law of Attraction? Then, use a the magic candle to draw the things you desire just by sending thanks and blessings to the Universe.

Use a candle of white color to show your appreciation to that person or set of life events. Each day, light the candle simultaneously and repeat the following words:

'(Name of the individual) I'm offering you a huge amount of appreciation

and best wishes

Let your heart fill with passion and love

Your dreams will be filled by peace

Your path will be illuminated with your Sunlight and Moonlight

Your life will be filled with joy in all ways'

You can also use this phrase to express thanks to the Universe in return

during times of crisis. Maybe you'd wish to maintain your overall health

or even to repair your or your relationship with someone you love. This could be any thing that you think of of. The candle is lit and you can speak the prayer to the white flame. In the light of the candle, you will be able to see

When the candle is lit, you can imagine your message bouncing up to the Universe and back down.

Easy love spell

The intention behind this spell is to bring greater love to your life. Nevertheless do not make a mental picture of any particular person while performing the ritual. We have explained that casting spells on others can alter their freedom of choice and is therefore strictly forbidden within Wicca.

It is necessary to have one white candle, and olive oil. Apply olive oil to the candle in a circular motion, beginning from the bottom, then after that, starting from the top. As you cleanse your candle using oil, fill the candle by imagining your feelings of love. Imagine the way you're in a an intimate relationship.

Once you're done, pick up your hammer and cut your desired design inside the candle.

For instance, "loving relationship", burn the candle, then place it safely but do not blow it out. It is recommended to perform this magical ceremony on the night of the Full Moon as well as the New Moon.

You are free to experiment in your work of magick and take whatever you think best for yourself as well as your magick. Your instincts will be the best source of information, since it is more instructive than every other book you've read.

Chapter 5: Simple Paper Magick

Written and spoken, have their own force. Like you've

We have learned that it is impossible to create a magical to cast a spell, invoke or chant.

without any words.

Unwritten rule of 'Be cautious': about what you'd like to happen may come to pass.

The meaning is read as literary by Witchcraft.

In order to perform magick with paper You will require an unfinished sheet of paper and then you select

whether it is blank white or colored either color or blank white paper. Additionally, you'll need either a pencil or a blank white paper.

You can use it only for magical uses and spells written by a spell writer candles with

the right the appropriate color.

You should put all your focus on the words you type. Write it

precisely how you would like exactly how you want it to be and make sure that you are specific about what you want to achieve and be specific about. It is important to define exactly what you want and how.

Use only honest claims.

As an example, "I'd like an opportunity to work in the field of advertising'

"I'd like healthy kidneys"

"I'd like to lose 5 pounds a week'

Don't use phrases like

"I'm not happy with this job. I'm looking for an alternative job"

"I'm unhappy with my hair. I would like stunning hair.'

"I'm in need of money!"

"I would like to be content.'

If you look at the last statements you can realize how absurd and confusing they are. It is possible to get different results or even no results even if you apply this kind of approach to Wicca.

Once you've finished this task, remove the sheet of paper and set the paper on fire. As it burns, you can consider the outcome you want to achieve or speak your thoughts out loud.

Another way to accomplish this magic is to put the paper in front of

A tree. Place it in the vicinity of an apple, oak pine, acacia, or even a cypress tree.

We thank the tree as well as your Elements of Earth for making your dreams come true.

Simple Magick for Banishing Negativity

All of us have experienced the ups and downs that come with life. In the majority of cases, negative moods do not last for lengthy, however if are stuck within a trance of negativity you should look at and gain control of your life. If you've got a reason to believe you have been manipulated by someone over you, don't immediately cast one to get it back. Be mindful of your Law of Three. If that is the case when someone has placed a curse over you or you're going through difficult times that you are experiencing, it's time to do an occult ritual that melts off all negative energy. The Elements will be there to assist anyone who would be willing to ask.

In order to work in conjunction with the element of flame it is necessary to use an ember. In this case, it's better to make use of a black candle.

Cleanse your mind first and relax as much as you possibly can. otherwise anger, negativity and frustrations can easily transfer through your body and affect your efforts.

Lighting the candle, imagine that it is a representation of the situation that you're seeking to resolve. Let it burn, and then think:

"Spirits of fire, take my advice and act as I would

Burn the candle, and then make the bad luck go away in me

My words are these

"So to speak, 'Move it on'

If you'd like to request Air for help in getting rid of negativity within your own life, get a piece of paper and begin writing about the challenging circumstance you're facing. Record everything you feel is not helping you achieve your objectives and living an enjoyable life. Once you're done burning the document, then throw the ashes to the air and call the air element Air to assist you:

"Power of wind and air

Burn these ashes away from me.

can harm no one so it's'

It is possible to harness the force of water to remove negative energy that is affecting your life This practice is ideal if you are near a lake, or rivers.

On an article of stone or paper write the things you would like to out, then walk towards the water and ask the element Water as you throw the paper into.

"Water spirits help me get rid of negative thoughts

And bad luck and misfortune and bad luck in my life you lose your water

could be that some of the things that are not benefit me remain far from my mind.

Spirits of water listen to my words, and then wash them away.

my bad luck to keep it from me, harm no one and follow my own rules

"So you're a good sport'

It is also possible to perform a ritual of bathing and, while doing it, invoke the water elements to cleanse the negative luck in your life. Imagine how all negative energy will be swept away.

Each time you decide to rid yourself of negative energy from your life, remember to give thanks to the universe for their assistance in the process.

Chapter 6: Divination Tools Used In Wicca

Through the ages, humans utilized various strategies in order to anticipate the future, anticipate hurricanes, and even to look at the historical past. It was the ability to sense that played a major factor in this. One thing worth noting prior to beginning is that everyone is gifted with psychic ability and the ability to sense. Intuition is what we all refer to as "that little voice inside our head".

The use of psychic powers was considered a taboo in the latter half of 20th century, and those who practice such things tend as being connected to something sinister.

It is what is actually happening, because those who make use of these powers, which are inherent for all human beings connect with their inner self as well as their spiritual self.

Witches and Wiccans are aware of the power of human spirit and are determined to develop their powers in tandem.

Witches use tools that are referred to as Divination tools. They're the instruments that allow you to connect with your intuition. These tools include tarot cards and oracle decks I CHing Oulja boards, Numerology, Pendulum etc.

Tarot cards

Tarot cards can be a powerful method of divination. Tarot cards are used by witches to forecast the future, make the right choices, and to use to help them grow spiritually. There is no need to be rushing to purchase these cards. You have to first figure out the type of card deck you're attracted to.

Tarot cards are split in Major Arcana (consisted of 22 cards) as well as Minor Arcana consisted of 56 cards.

Major Arcana represents spiritual growth The Major Arcana represents spiritual development, and every card symbolizes spirituality's path. Choose each card examine it, and then try to figure out the meaning behind the card on your own.

Major Arcana The Minor Arcana represents the four elements.

Cups are the symbol of "Water"

Wands are a symbol of the fire.

Sword is a symbol of 'Air'

Pentacle is a symbol of the 'Earth'

Make use of your tarot deck whenever you are prompted to make use of them. It is possible to use them when conducting rituals, or spread cards to get the messages from the spiritual realms. Make sure you clean them often, especially when they've been utilized by someone else.

- Numerology

Researchers have proven that all things within the Universe is a reflection of its own frequency and energy. The power of numbers to create a more accurate perception of their own lives, the path they take and their destiny.

As as a Wiccan take advantage of tapping into the future of your life and your fellow Wiccans' future with the help of Numerology. Numerology will help you overcome difficult individuals and situations that arise in your daily life. Numerology is extremely useful for a way to deal with difficult situations.

What are the significance of the numbers 1-9:

Number 1: Leadership' Courage; Independent.

Color - Red. Stone: Ruby; Sign: Aries.

Number 2: Gentle; Harmonious; Cooperative.

Color: Orange and Gold; Stone: Moonstone' Sign: Libra.

Number 3: Self - Expression; Enthusiastic; Optimistic.

Color: Yellow; Stone: Topaz. Sign: Leo.

#4: Solid, hardworking and practical.

Color: Green; Stone: Emerald; Sign: Taurus.

Number 5: Communicative: Risk taking; Youthful

Color: Turquoise; Stone: Turquoise and Aquamarine; Sign: Gemini.

6. Family; Responsibility: Serving others.

Color: Royal blue. Sapphire; Sapphire and Sign Libra.

Number 7: Solitary; Mystical; Inventor

Color: Violet; Stone: Amethyst; Sign: Virgo.

Number 8: Power; Achievement; Organization

Color: Pink; Stone; Rose Quartz; Sign: Capricorn.

Number 9: Competition; Spiritual; Forgiveness.

Color: White; Stone: Opal; Sign:Scorpio.

- Pendulum

The practice was used in the ancient civilisations that were found in Greece, Rome and Persia. Pendulums are very well-liked among Witches and is a breeze to make. It is possible to make your own pendulum using an item of jewelry, or even a crystal that is hung on strings. But before you use the pendulum, determine the significance of each direction prior to seeking answers. Watch the pendulum perform its work.

- Oulja Board

"The Oulja Board (/'wi:dZ@/ WEE-j@)) is often referred to as the board of spirits. The Oulja Board is a place where you can write the alphabet's letters as well as numbers from 0 through 9, and words such as "Yes", "No", "Hello" and "Goodbye". The board is accompanied by small pieces made of plastic or wood as moveable in order to convey the spirit's message by writing the word on the table. The technique is also referred to as channeling.

It is a skill that only few people are able to master, because it demands a lot of psychic capabilities. For you to utilize Oulja Board Oulja Board properly, you should not be scared of encounters with the spirit world. They are not harmful or harm you in any way. However should you feel concerned by their presence, it is best to take the board off your desk and avoid using it for any time. Prior to beginning your séance begin to visualize a bright, strong illumination coming from the sky, around your. In this way, you're protected from negativity.

- Runes

The Runes alphabet is a classic which was widely used for centuries by Germans, Scandinavians and Anglo and Scandinavians and Anglo-Saxons. The belief is that every word of this alphabet is associated with magical significance. Every letter in the Runes Alphabet is inscribed on wood, or on a table that is made from clay.

You are free to create your own runes using clay, and writing each letter on tables. Use runes like you use tarots. Distribute them, and then read the message they convey. There are a variety of famous spreads:

The spread of the single rune will give you the solution to your query

The Norns spread provides you with a overview of your history as well as the present and future.

The Diamond spread can be a great source of immediate benefits.

The circle spread provides an indication of two individuals.

No matter what tool you select be aware that it's linked to the rest of the devices you make use of. Take care of them, wash them often and constantly strive to understand better the way they function.

Chapter 7: Walking The Path Of Wicca And Being A Witch

So far in the past and now you're keen on becoming an Witch and pursuing the way of Wicca. It could seem like an easy and exciting thing to pursue But don't jump to a conclusion right now. There are obligations and personal obligations you need to know about. This book provides a wealth of information However, it is imperative to commit yourself to additional books, in order to expand your understanding of Wicca. It will teach you in greater details about rituals, deities as well as holidays and covens and about being a single Wiccan, the practice of magick, historical of spells, magick, nature and the elements. Once you have more information about Wicca, you'll be able to tell your own self if Wicca is the path that you wish to follow within your daily life.

Being a witch are expected to fulfill many obligations such as taking care of Nature and all living things that you encounter. Learn to become capable of joining the coven. Be respectful of the beliefs of others and do not make your beliefs a burden on anyone else. There is a chance that you will be tempted to be a part of Wicca at some point, but you shouldn't try to forcibly force family and friends to join the coven against their own will.

Following the path of Wicca and leading the life of the life of a Witch is a challenge that requires courage to make changes in your lifestyle. If you've made your choice and are determined to lead a life of an Witch One of the first actions you must take is face your inner self and accept the dark side of you.

The role of a Witch is primarily focused on self-awareness, being able to acknowledge your own truth and look back on the past.

This is essential in the process of making changes and becoming better at what you do. One of the essential aspects that a witch must have is the silence. It is important to avoid becoming emotionally involved, and it will happen when you grow, develop and become better at the craft. Be silent about the work you do. It is important to be conscious of the destructive power of your Ego when it is not in check. If it's not kept in the dark then it's not really magic at all.

Utilize your energy effectively and work magick that can help to make the our world a better place. Everyone is aware of the destruction that humanity is bringing upon itself as an Witch you are a catalyst for positive changes, no matter how small changes may occur. Participate in the emergence of the sun on this globe.

The last thing to do is be confident in your talents. Trust in yourself as well as the route you've chosen, and your magical work. Incorporate your desire to create an improved world by combining your own energy and factors. This way, you will be able to produce and perform beautiful magick work.

Chapter 8: What Does Witch Mean?

Witches are available in various sizes and ages, as well as hues and even characters. They're experts as software engineers, educators as well as barkeeps, landscapers and airline Stewards. Someone who cuts your hair or repairs your car might be witch. They can be female or male--no, the male witch doesn't qualify as an actual warlock. He might explode if believe that he is considering the present circumstances. Warlock is derived from the Old English word signifying "vow breaker" or "liar."

It's a fact that reading this book suggests that you believe you too, have some potential. Be prepared for the unexpected. There is always a chance. With a little planning, you'll be able to show your power to the world and learn how to make use of it to influence your destiny.

WHY IS WITCHCRAFT GAINING FAME TODAY?

The witchcraft of today is significant because it tackles the major problems of our time: respect for the planet as well as sexual orientation fairness in addition to overcoming rigid predispositions as well as extremist logic. The practice also enlivens those who follow this path to develop their unique abilities so they can take responsibility for their own lives and live the life that they choose to be.

Most witches are seeking to grow their own humanity and themselves in general and remain in sync with all the world. This implies working for the more prominent significant--regularly using magic--and hurting none. In addition, it means taking responsibility in your actions, thoughts and actions because everything you do affects all other things.

Once you have figured out the best way to use your everyday talents as witches and a witch, you'll discover the possibility of a whole new universe of possibilities for outcomes is available. It is possible to apply what's known as "the" Law of Attraction to improve your financial situation, the quality of your relationships, well-being, and overall happiness. Also, you'll have the capacity to aid other people. You'll also gain the visibility of your status to the world. Magic can't aid in finishing a task to finish work or school assignments, nor raise your height or help fix a damaged tire. However it may help strengthen your mental and physical receptivity as well as fixation to others, and increase your appeal to other people, or draw people to you that can solve the problem?

It's smart to slow down in the beginning-- similar to how you'd do on the off possibility of training for a race that was long distance. So, you can enjoy yourself and avoid any accidents.

WITCHCRAFT AND MODERNITY

In the last few months, Rowlands as well as Warnier 1988 (also known as Fisiy as well as Rowlands 1989) In addition, given more momentum in the late 1990s The investigation into 'African witchcraft' has seen an easy revival. It has also been accompanied by innovative methodological, theoretical and even topical twists. Like all developments, they are occurring one after each other in the context of human studies constant concern to make sense' witchcraft. As anthropologists, they are also seeking greater vigor than ever before in the past - ways to challenge the west's teleology of social changes.

One of the most significant disputes which has been recurrently being discussed is because the forces behind witchcraft, they're able to easily and without an effort re-evaluate their position in various situations: "It is unambiguously through this internal conflict that occult discussions can so successfully consolidate the current changes' . Witchcraft, therefore, is a dynamic phenomenon and is a part of the global community and, as such, is often portrayed as a contemporary. The modernity of witchcraft is usually presented as an examination of earlier experts who, like Levy-Bruhl said, believed that witchcraft should be primitive and prelogical, or, as earlier anthropologists frequently suggested that it was a static and narrowly defined convention. This is a fact that previous researchers distorted witchcraft because they did not look beyond the smallest, city network at the level of. Finally, in light of the dynamic nature of witchcraft, as well as its constant engagement with current day time this grant included the credibility of rituals and witchcraft discussions for the reason that they're always altering, and enduring to the vital cycles of our world in long periods of time. Longue duree. This volume exposes how close-up images of occult and barbarian powers within Sierra Leone are both generally well-educated and up to date, as well as the way these images have frequently replicated themselves in continuous local, trans-local conversations over decades. In addition to being concerned with the authentic method, Fixity and Geschiere problematize the link between witchcraft and progress within Cameroon through the 60s until the present day, and show how the local understanding of witchcraft has changed significantly from 'leveling' towards "aggregation.' There have been many occasions, more favorable locations, and in a variety of methods, the occult and modernity have merged.

The claims that late-breaking researchers are making regarding witchcraft, namely that it's current and not customary and that it is a wide-ranging phenomenon, not just a neighborhood and chronicled, not static are all important. There are instances where it is equally important to note that these instances are not completely novel regardless of whether they're infrequently displayed in the way they are. In the earlier segment, previous historians of anthropology were concerned with witchcraft due to changes in society and worked to purify witches in a variety of ways. These developments were anticipated in the area of growing and spread of witchcraft. Furthermore, even though the data might suggest that some previous works were centered on the town however, some also were based on the occult and were rehearsed in urban environments as well as at rural urban interstices. The ongoing investigation has been criticized for having as their starting and closing the town as their small microcosmos.

It is a general moment, I believe that witchcraft, at least for a few Anthropologists, is partially incorporated into the modern world, or at least part of it.

Anthropologists have, for long recognized that witchcraft does not suffer in the age of'modernity'. Truth is, and because they've seen it as frequently as they can that witchcraft, as well as other occult beliefs and practices are often subjected to "opposing" modifications and then redesigned in response to changing circumstances. This is why it's not a good idea to suggest that, as many sociologists have done claimed, that modernity has destroyed custom or causes the secularization of.

The recent attacks on witchcraft do not merely repeat the things that have already been discussed. In the current dangerous debate, it has been extremely in certain ways and gives a new possibilities to our previous knowledge of witchcraft. The reason that the late witchcraft researchers differ from their predecessors isn't their focus on social changes or believing that witchcraft can be a response to change in society, but they insist that witchcraft be essential to the modern world as it's modern, but essential to modernity.

A recent development that signals an important shift in current methods to combat witchcraft is the idea of modernity, which is being sent. When arguing the idea that witchcraft is modern and relevant, it is appropriate to recognize the fact that modernity's facets are diverse and that occult and witchcraft beliefs, as well as rehearses, are in tune to different modernist directions. According to Bastian asks in her discussion on the cosmological aspects of Nigerian contemporaryity: 'Can people's have experiences of living in the present have any chance of being homogeneous if their social orders, chronicles and the underlying cosmological concepts don't have the same meaning to each other? The issue has been posed in a series of ways - not just by those who are studying witchcraft and the result is dismantling teleologies.This can be done through a number of different methods. It helps to understand the lack of assemblies across the world the fact that modernity does not conform to one particular arrangement or follow a specific course. In the short term, it's certain that the modern world is all everywhere'. The world is "all over the place" the reality we live in hasn't had one and appears to be highly unlikely to ever get one.

One reason is this. Considering the ongoing poststructuralist concerns about majorities, fracture and telos, a variety of scholars have advocated the idea of a 'different' contemporary'.

Modernity does not have a singular implicit telos or justification for the modern age, if it was ever an element in itself and has taken numerous and often unexpected directions. The idea of accepting different forms of contemporary trends is to assume that to observe the world as a result of the constant construction and reconstitution of many social initiatives. The notion of multiple mothers is a clear rejection of the 1950s and 60s modernization theories, as well as the speculations on reliance that all rely on to see a cultural, and eventually term, global combination. This dispels the mythology about globalization, which incorrectly suggests the world as a whole; and it detonates the myth of globalization that incorrectly suggests the world in the age of modernity. be able to have one. Even more accommodating to the idea of a different era draws the social theories together on questions of differences, heterogeneity important and diverse imbalances and discusses the role of power. It is easy to take into consideration globalization and the underlying inequality that is created by it but without the assumption that we are getting one.

Because modernity isn't a catalyst for the dispersion of cultures and social order It isn't surprising that there's nothing particularly 'normal and inexplicably different in it. Modernity doesn't have to be the consequence of a inevitably change in the structure and thought. Maybe, the modernization process may have been a result of cultural change for a long time. It is interesting to think about different maternities at this point can be helpful in reminding us that our imagined realistic speech is formulated with a specific language which means the idea that "we are one of the others" It allows the modernist to question its own ethos: by recognizing it as an extremely cultural undertaking as well as to consider its instances with a sense of fairness, not just as normal reality, but rather as specific discussions about what is real and requires clarification.

Modernity being viewed as a social project has allowed anthropologists concerned about witchcraft, to put together our own scientific reflections to ourselves and find parallels to the activities of "occult economics" all over the globe. In the process the process has opened the theoretical space to the self-study. The focus has moved to certain aspects of intense and how the shrouded forces create regular universes within certain cultural systems. The comparison between the west and the other cultures - with regards to the paranoid and witchcraft of children, abuse and evil custom spirits ownership within Asia as well as American professionals as having similar opinions about world events are significant as it proves that "witchcraft," and the unique nature of the intensity that it reveals can be more than just African wonders.

They function flawlessly in design all everywhere, even they are characterized by different contemporary and styles of culturally curved designs. Furthermore, through rendering these beliefs and designs in a parallel fashion many ongoing researches have suggested that 'occult economy examine the shifting contemporaryity they create sections. It is important to note that this particular endeavor allowed anthropologists do things that have been long over expectations, which is to make nature the new 'other' which is a way of turning our traditional western society on its ear.

The significance of this motive certainly is that the concept of 'occult' economies aren't without their challenges. In the case of a particular thing like Sally Falk Moore (1999) suggested, the notion of the occult is incredibly broad. The question is about what assumptions would one be able to talk about and dissect these different events and wonders in a different way? Another issue is how these approaches can be interpreted to make a false connection between modernity and the occult. Modernity as a concept and having a connection to modernity is not in any way equivalent. Does witchcraft, or the occult more providing an examination of modernity and globalization? Should it be as? Are witchcraft primarily about symbolic political issues? If so, is it possible that anthropologists tell an established liberal narrative by focusing on 'others', and in the process, inscribe the very 'us and 'them' divisions which we seek to deconstruct? It is nearly impossible to say that everywhere and in every situation there are people who oppose or studying the developments and adaptations to modernization and surely they're far from the business relations that are expected to lead these. What many people seek is the indigenization and modernization of society They have cultural spaces within the larger scheme of everything. At the end of the day, we must give careful attention to the practice of witchcraft in particular contexts, both in recorded and social instead of expecting huge consequences. If we're able to effectively dispel one of the most important modern ace tales - the one of uniplanar development it is important not to fall into the trap of allowing ourselves to be manipulated by the other.

WITCHCRAFT AND GLOBALIZATION

The latest investigations into witchcraft, the expanding of an extent in notable words has been brought about with a broadening of the scope within geological contexts, which has led to a shift in scope of the investigation. In the meantime, investigation condemn fundamental functionalists for limiting their research to local instances, and also for claiming that witchcraft is solely the consequence of a specific, narrow societies like the Azande. It is a rebuke, especially on the extent of investigation and suggests that the past centuries or didn't go far enough to respond to the concerns they raised, or the questions they raised were only marginally admonished from the very beginning. This raises questions about the past cases that have suggested that witchcraft beliefs are likely flourish in small enclosed gatherings where the ability to move within and outside is constrained when the group is inevitably close and jobs are not well defined or so defined in a way that they're difficult to fulfill. From a modern perspective, the witchcraft is a part of the larger cultural context; it's constructed, or perhaps even transmitted by trans-local "others," as well as images that are a part of how it relates to an vastly diverse universe of values and interpretations. It has led researchers to carry out ethnography in an unbalanced way that runs unrestrictedly, starting by examining one aspect and moving on to the next including issues at the neighborhood level, legislative matters as well as links to the urban country with the state of the nation and the international system. The expanding expository skylines resulted in the need about the global interstices between neighborhoods.

Within this vast universe of important importance, some claim that witchcraft may be viewed as an indigenous-shaped evaluation of the maternities) as well as private business and globalization, as well as the intrinsically dangerous relationships of creation associated with them. In this way it isn't only a matter of being caught into and created in the world system but it is more according to individuals who have conducted investigations, and provides the reader a Meta editorial on the ill actions of free enterprise and globalization.

In any case how is this environment any different than past times? Is there a distinct break, an evident record of a break from the past? It seems like there is something totally different in our current world, due to the rapid development of products, people and the thoughts of people around the globe. Yet, at the same time there are incontrovertible patterns in our world that we must be extremely mindful of not overstate the complexity across a long period as well as today, dynamic and static limitless and unlimited as it is to reinforce those very concepts that Anthropologists have attempted to instill doubt over. One of the major concerns for social scientists was how to grasp the current world of majority diverse modernity, constantly increasing cultural streams, as well as ever-growing pressures on powers of heterogeneity as well as homogeneity. Witchcraft has a connection with this issue, argue ongoing researchers, as it is often the outcome of interconnected processes of data people, goods and individuals.

NORMAL MISCONCEPTIONS ABOUT WITCHES

Before proceeding further before we do anything else, let us get rid of the absurd notions that a handful of people hold concerning witches. Witches are portrayed as a threat to humanity through ignorance and fear. In a significant amount of time, traditional religious beliefs have favored negative images of witches. During a time called "The Burning Times," this false belief led to many guilty people across Europe as well as the New World. At times there is a constant stream of media with a deceitful portrayal of witches and magical creatures which further confuses the matter. To clarify:

Fairies don't eat or take care of children, the idea comes from the old tales which were often believed to be doing so.

Witches aren't Satanists that offer their spirit to the devil as an outcome of various forces. Witches who have a plethora of ashes don't believe in Satan He's an Christian Origination.

The witches aren't riding on sweepers; they travel in cars as well as airplanes, trains, and cars just like any person else. (You might see a security sticker which reads "I'm driving this vehicle because my floor brush's in the shop," but it's just a joke.) Pizza is the preferred food of witches over those who are new to them rapidly.

The witches do not acquire magical abilities from strange predecessors and even it's possible that Grandma used to be a witch, and taught you the Craft in your youth You'll be able to get an advantage over fellow witches who are aspiring to become. Some witches don't possess extraordinary mystic abilities and they don't have the ability to predict. There are mystics who could be witches and a lot of witches develop their intuition by studying. However, in reality you believe in mystics, everyone is a witch and that includes the person you are.

Witches aren't a part of or battle evil spirits such as vampires, zombies or even other monsters. They are better at their actions. Some witches don't believe in gods or goddesses from the past. Some are skeptical of any form of god. They don't last forever; they have average lives, just similar to other individuals.

They aren't awe-inspiring old witches They can also be stunningly beautiful and youthful However most of them are healthy people similar to us.

The witches aren't involved in fights or conflicts with the other magicians. Witches from Salem, Massachusetts, for instance, aren't in an ongoing battle to New Orleans' voodoo priestesses. If you choose to transform into the witch you'll need be able to throw away all of the absurd and thrilling things that you've heard, seen and have read about witchcraft. For your time you'll have to deal and be constantly irritated by the insanity of people who may never think of offending people of color, Jews, or different individuals as much as witches. Just put on your witchy protective shield, and go in the process of rehearsing your original content.

Wizards, Sorcerers, and Magicians

The term "magician" and "wizard" are a reference to woman or man. Wizard comes from the word meaning "insightful," and alchemist is a reference to "witch" or "seer." Magicians are also suitable to both genders, witches and sexes as everything is the same. In accordance with the culture that the word magician was used to describe people skilled in crystal gazing divination, witchcraft casting spells, other magic-related expressions.

In this publication it will use some phrases over and over. We can clarify a few by asking for an orderly distance from chaos:

Witches makes use of their abilities in tandem with normal laws of nature in order to alter the reality according to their own desires.

Witchcraft refers to the practice of managing energy with various intentions in order to achieve a desired final.

Magic refers to the transformation that takes place when a witch or magician manipulates energy using techniques that are supernatural. It is the "k" toward the finish of the universe can recognize magic as it is and stage deceiving (or clever deception).

When you look around we will see that witches use a variety of techniques and utilize a lot of strategies during performing their craft. Additionally, they perform various forms of magic to satisfy a variety of motives. When you study the art of the witch, and figure out the best way to use your own magic abilities to discover the one that suits your needs and the direction you'd like to bring into your own journey.

Chapter 9: Witchcraft And Religion

As with people from diverse cultures, witches are able to share some ideas but are different from some others. We'll explore the various aspects of this in the coming days. Their thinking may be influenced by their culture's traditions and their foundations, personal life interactions, or personal personalities. It's okay. It is not necessary to be plugged an exact method of conviction or rules in order to qualify as an witch.

In the past, many witches engaged on their own specialties as an integral part of the family customs where they had to be meticulously ready, similar to how others could learn brickwork, carpentry, or even carpentry. Towns were a "sly society" to whom residents sought out a vast array of support such as urging yields grow to repairing a damaged heart. Repairing was a major portion of the work done by witches as well as a lot of witches had a background as botanists or experts in maternity. For such services it is possible for the witch to receive chickens, some portion of grains, or other needs.

The idea of religion was not a part of witchcraft in itself however, individual witches often accepted the opinions of their family or the culture. It's the same to us today. If you're associated in a certain religion or follow a specific religious way of life, don't abandon it in order to transform into the role of a witch. There is a possibility of integrating the beliefs of your religion to your magic practice. If you do not adhere to any particular belief system it's fine too. Witches are free to follow any faith and on the other hand, there is no religion at all. Due to the lack of creeds, rules, or a religious affiliation isn't a reason to say that witches aren't morally.

Witchcraft has become a commonplace. This isn't a prediction but rather a description of the current state. In this book, a lot of this process has already happened, and the rest unfolds under our noses. The speed at the improvement that has occurred is quite remarkable. As opposed to the normal speed of changes recorded this has been nearly immediately. While it was created thirty years in order to establish the method that the state of view towards Witchcraft could be flipped in less than 10 years. It happened so fast that if one knew the things to look on, you can see the event unfold.

Rapid changes that are crucial are difficult to make adjustments to and are much more difficult to comprehend. If we were to consider them to constitute a significant part of an overall image, will we be in a position to move and away enough from them to comprehend the significance of them? It is possible to begin by asking two questions:

1.) What does this progression indicate for the ultimate fate of the present Witchcraft as well as the Neopagan advancement?

2.) What are they implying in the end for our country and our style to live?

In the year 1965, Pennethorne Hughes, a British professional regarding the background of history behind Witchcraft stated that Witchcraft is a fading mythology. The belief was, "passing on quickly" and was influenced by mainstream media as well as the well-known and popular training that it received, along with the incredible realism of overall growth. In the words of Hughes, "Witchcraft as a religion of a faction within Europe has gone out of fashion. It was a kind of ripeness-based conviction that is crude, mixing the most timely and enlightening insights, the course is over. The reason Hughes's misguidedness hilarious is the fact that in 1965 the counterculture as well as Neopaganism had just begun to find their wings as well. British Wicca is at this moment spotting a fertile spot for growth within The United States. Of course it is true that the "specialists" tend to be the first to look for anything that doesn't fit the presumptions of their ability.

In all likelihood, since Hughes has announced the end of his tenure in the past, modern-day Witchcraft has seen only progress and progress. The Neopagan growth, which was initiated by the modern Witchcraft and has seen numerous successes and leaps forward over the last 35 years. This is true both socially as well as politically. This has not been without loss, of course but Witches have also been subject to a great deal of restrictions and a hostile image as a result of the process. In the end, in the ever-changing "culture war," the conclusion is that Neopaganism was not at the bottom of any major fight they have fought. There have been a few legitimate conflicts which have erupted en way have resulted in victories for the Witches too.

With this kind of success in its portfolio It is not a surprise that Neopaganism has a steady and expansive state of mind. The Neopagans are extremely conscious of how people's attitudes are changing and feel that the changes in society will open new opportunities for them to grow and develop. The kind of dangerous event Witchcraft faced in the late 1990s has more to do with the circumstances, it also brings challenges.

MODERN-DAY WITCHCRAFT'S TWO CULTURES

This is the very first place that it's created, and if it is not a crisis in character or, at the very least it's a case of character confusion in the process of process of development. Prior to 1996, Neopagan movement was dominated by the rigid Witches who believed that they were as being a part of a broader separation of their "unremarkable" world and the whole of its (Christian-based) properties, structures as well as exercises. However, the advent in The Craft set off the ascendance of popular culture Witchcraft in a way that was actually the middle of the road. It brought a flood of brand new Witches with no stake of the social world that traditional Witches had in common. The mainstream society Witches generally were not a part of any "inception" or any sort of preparation for the occult; they were not associated with any conventions or instruction that they could not or wouldn't be a part of existing groups They were completely in the world of ordinary people without any sense of separation from it aside from having a strong attitude towards society in general.

The divide between the traditional Witchcraft and modern society Witchcraft was almost a symbiosis from the beginning. The newly-formed Witches didn't receive much assistance from the traditional in the event that they were associated with one or the existing associations it was likely that they would be get thrown out. The old-fashioned, insofar they were concerned were scared by the legal risks of managing children, as well as being beware of the group of fashionable witches that were chattering without thinking and without duty or even knowing. The division in that moment was heightened, because young Witch wanted to be had no alternative but to create their notions of Witchcraft from what they were watching on TV or via the Internet or simply by talking to their friends.

It has led to form two distinct and distinct communities within the overall category in "present-day Witchcraft." "Conventional" culture "conventional" culture incorporates the Witches who believe that it should be a process of recovery or endurance or the re-evaluation of established beliefs and practices (for instance, the beliefs Gerald Gardner professed to have been able to discover in 1939) They also typically believe that their beliefs are "strict." The history of this particular culture was covered in Chapter Eight and the development to the present standard takes place through interfaith efforts and adhering to the strict and non-religious. Their goal in efforts to mainstream is acceptance as a legitimate faith, in line with the legal and social norms.

"Mainstream society" Witchcraft, in contrast, is less influenced by a certain culture or tradition and less inclined to believe itself as "strict." It was founded in 1996. mainstream society Witchcraft has not yet been 10-years-old as at the time of writing but is currently being shaped by the powerhouses which brought it into existence. New Witch magazine could be seen as the journalistic voice of society's mainstream Witchcraft and its commercial bazaar. It is filled with ads, including the ones that advertise Snapdragon gifts ("Nothing is mundane") as well as Mystic treasures Clothier ("Cloak Yourself in Mystery") as well as reviews of books, articles and other publications. The majority of the time, New Witch displays an appearance of Witchcraft that isn't necessarily an actual "religion," however, and also as an "way of life," which is bolstered by the information that is scattered throughout the magazine in "strict" language.

NEW WITCH: IDOL-MAKING IN THE MODERN WORLD

A recurring spread in The magazine reveals how popular society Witchcraft is a mix of excessive admiration and fascination. The piece, which is titled "Summoning Buffy -- Discovering the Magic of Pop Icons," is a step-by-step guide to create symbols for the mind. The author acknowledges that there are people who might be a bit sarcastic about using the characters of television as "gods," however he does not believe in critics ("conventional" Witches?) in his one and only mention of the following:

Many magicians resent the use of mainstream society in the pursuit of magick. But, as a matter of fact I believe that the mainstream culture can be a powerful media for magick. The most popular society icon could be transformed into a receptive central point of magick. Buffy The Vampire Slayer, makes a real-life role model.

The creator at this is able to explain the way Buffy (or any other fictional characters) is able to be turned into a functioning "god structure" for use in custom occult. Based on a theory that is common in Neopagans, a "divine being structure" is created in an "higher plane" when enormous numbers of people empty their convictions in their collective thoughts of what or who gods or goddesses can be. This "god structure" that individuals construct in this way take into account a fact that is higher than those who create it. If more people have confidence in the "god structure," and the more faith they place on it, the more powerful it becomes "god structure" becomes. In this way, a popular icon such as Buffy or, at the very least over a few long time periods becomes a vessel to store the emotional power of the admiration of her followers; in changing the Buffy persona into one's personal "god structure," one is able to benefit from that stored energy to use it to serve enchanted ends. At that the point of disclosure, explains the exact method of doing this by laying out a series of paths for readers to take.

Once you're entangled to the viewpoint of the creator's view of the universe His instructions are positive. With no benefit of this viewpoint, however the case, they seem to be a sloppy, petty statement. allow us to imagine rubbish, in the best case scenario, or the risk of a dangerous and twisted gibberish, at a minimum. Whatever the case may be the text does reflect three aspects:

1.) It is a glimpse of how mainstream society views Witchcraft has gotten to;

2.) It illustrates the distinctions between the mainstream of society Witchcraft as well as traditional witchcraft "customary" kind just as similar;

3.) The manner that this approach is able to increase recognition this day demonstrates how unsettling the state of the general public has been transformed into a frenzied appreciation.

RELIGION AND THE TWO CULTURES OF WITCHCRAFT

"Summoning Buffy" is a representation of society's mainstream Witchcraft throughout the process of in the process of developing and an esoteric. It is alarming due to its utterly insignificantness as well as its casual vandalism of ideas and images and the orderly absence of care for anything that does not belong to oneself, and only for self. In addition, the call for spiritual existences that involve "tracing out" and "tuning in to your god" is simple. These items, as obnoxious as they could be, are merely features of human fallibility that have been heightened, enhanced and enhanced for use in the present and transmitted by techniques for the current media. "Conjuring Buffy" is not at all (or is not exactly) real-life representation of human nature today and has been reduced to a simple animation.

The fact that mainstream society believes Witchcraft is a re-creation of the human inclination to fall is something it shares to the most part with various forms of agnosticism that are as old in the current day. In the event that "Conjuring Buffy" diminishes otherworldliness in the pursuit of and using power, it only brings an essential issue with faith-based agnosticism in the first place. C. S. Lewis identified polytheism as "the eternal commonality that is inherent to the human hearth

Neopaganism is a type of this "changeless common tendency," and is a part of mainstream society. Witchcraft is one of the ways that is influenced by the modern society that is stripped down and speedy. "Summoning Buffy" shows what the meaning of agnosticism is in the absence of compromises and interruptions. Create a divine entity and go through it. eliminate the idea.

WITCHES AND CHRISTIANS

The Witches I've by and in come into contact with have generally have been "conventional," "strict" Witches and adherents of Gardnerian Wicca, alongside its affiliates and branches. After a few minutes of speaking with these Witches looking through their publications and books as well as their websites and in general trying to get their viewpoint, I am inclined to believe that they are calling their "religion" at face esteem. Today's Witchcraft is in fact an "made up" religion, but at the time there are many modern faiths. The modern age of Witchcraft is completely off base in its social and cultural stance, making it physically dangerous to me However, as (in my judgment) there are many religionswhich are not as ancient as current ones. From a scriptural perspective each and every human "religion" is truly misguided efforts to attain God by means of its own or in any way (and as such, it is "made up"), therefore, over the course of time their differences appear more obvious than real. If Mormonism as well as Scientology could be "religions," it is difficult to establish the legitimacy of closing down the school to contemporary Witchcraft. If I, as an Christian could delve in to a contemplated and kind "discourse" with somebody who is not a believer in God (a Buddhist) and with someone who believes in the God of the elephants (a Hindu) and an God of good and bad karma (a Hindu) for what reasons would I not be offended by having a similar conversation with someone who believe the nature of God (a Witch)? But, a lot of Christians avoid any possibility. They'd create some painful impressions by treating the Witch in the same way that they'd treat an Buddhist or Mormon during a general discussion or in the role of a close neighbors. Another reason behind this hesitation is that many Christians are mistakenly identifying the modern day Witchcraft by referring to the offensive stereotypes of the medieval Witchcraft. However the simple act of resolving the feeling of numbness doesn't suffice to get it to go away. There's a conflict between Christianity as well as modern-day Witchcraft which is real and is not based on misconception, even if it's often misinterpreted. More than just the mere "pressure" among Christianity and Witchcraft There is an inside-out battle over their distinct goals to be more aware and get social. These two visions are imperfect but to the extent the one is successful within us while the other is slowed down. There's a difficult element of the unnatural conflict between Witches and Christians which cannot be cured through any level of instruction or defeat with any kind of kindness. My experience in "discourse" (both formal and informal) and Neopagans has persuaded me about a particular thing that is genuine respect and gratitude. can be developed between Witches as well as Christians in a unique way but only if the two groups can see the elements of disagreement between their members, and then agree to put them in a tangential to the side to "we'll let history choose those issues," to make an alliance that is possible. It requires more effort to build trust, mutual respect and compassion as opposed to the typical relationship, but it is certainly likely - assuming that both parties must be able to.

Christians have become accustomed to the idea of regret We are not be afraid by numbness or off-putting actions of the Church as well as in the present The more important issue is the difficulty of separating real bad behavior from snarky stories and unsubstantiated allegations. The most troubling aspect could be the inability of the current Witches to realize that the bulk of their beliefs are based upon a hostile Christian prejudice, and that their preference is founded on desecration and total deceit. It is interesting that those Witches that are most likely to confront this aspect of their history are the "conventional," "strict"

Witches as opposed to the more counter Christian attitudes of the Witchcraft Charter Myth thrive over the uppermost ranks of mainstream society "way of life" Witches. In any case, there are three motives behind this differentiating factor:

1.) A strict Witches tend to be progressively shrewd and becoming "genuine" individuals who care about matters such as the truthfulness of their claims as well as the legitimacy of their beliefs in the context of the general public; they are likely to remain more attentive to the recurring grant which discredits those who believe in"the" Charter Myth;

2.) As the years pass as time passes, more and more people fall towards rigid Witchcraft because it demands the individual terms and not just for the disavowal of Christianity but also for its aversion to Christianity.

3.) In line with as a strict Witchcraft rules, this is usually via interfaith associations, coexistence together with Christians and Christianity is now a common everyday practice for increasing numbers of faithful Witches.

WITCHCRAFT AND ANTI-CHRISTIANITY

If there is a legitimate discussion between Witches and Christians both sides have to acknowledge that both sides are confined in their basic ways. Christians are able to provide their own philosophical explanation to this issue However, from a purely religious perspective there is a reason to believe that Witchcraft's battle against the modernity of Christianity is essential for its historical starting point and also to its internal self-portrait. The opponent of Christian thought is embedded in the fake history Gerald Gardner imagined tying his "Wicca" back to medieval Witchcraft as well as the ancient Goddess-favor. One aspect of the battle opposition to Christianity is inseparable from the socially rebellious character of the entire project so that the manner of living the man was subverting is based on Christianity.

Wicca and Witchcraft

Some people confuse the words witch as well as Wicca. Witchcraft is a method and a skill, it is an approach to using energy to produce results. Wicca is a religious method of thinking that comes which is characterized by its code of ethics and ideals, as well as rituals, gods, and so on. In fact, many witches living in the West nowadays consider themselves Wiccan or Wiccan, and Wiccans mostly use witchcraft. But witches aren't Wiccan.

Different Worlds of Existence

A lot of witches recognize that at least one world that are not ours exist, and that nonphysical beings have shared the universe with us. Certain people believe in individual gods or goddesses. Witches of different types communicate of angels, holy messengers, and even nature spirits. Some believe that everything in the world--earth, stone, creatures, or plants-- possesses an exceptional quality or soul. However, witches don't require faith in the divine beings that carry the game, in just the same way in the way that software engineers, circuit testers and dental Hygienists do not have to adhere to an individual faith in order in order to fulfill their duties.

LIFE AFTER DEATH AND REINCARNATION

The process of passing through birth and life is well-known to everyone but for certain witches, it isn't over. Instead of life ending after death, when the body dies the witches believe that a person's spirit, soul, or energy of the individual goes on into a realm beyond physical existence and could ultimately and be revived in a different body, in a different and space. A large majority of them view Earth as an "school" and accept we have come to earth as students who be taught. The cycle continues until the soul has gone through all the tasks the intention was to study. When the cycle is complete and the spirit is ready to go back to a state of bliss and healing.

The idea isn't unique for witches. Christians, Muslims, and those of various faiths believe that our spirits will continue to exist even after we die as well. Hindus have believed in Rebirth for centuries.

Where Do Witches Go When They Die?

Christianity is a religion with a heaven. Buddhism offers Nirvana. Where are witches going after they have bitten the dust? There are many Wiccans believe the idea that their spirits are taken into the Summerland to rest, which is a place of repose before rebirth as new bodies. This is the continuous sequence of birth death, resurrection, and passing.

The Witch's Connection to Nature

Despite their distinct opinions and the particular methods used to rehearse their particular style, the current witches have a few commonalities. The most prominent is their respect to Nature. It includes respecting the Earth adapting themselves to the cycles of her seasons as well as tapping into the power of nature to perform magical tasks.

Much like shamans, witches think of their bodies as an actual substance. their own home, which they respect and protect, not an area to conquer and take over. They see the natural world, animals and all that is on the planet as educators as part of a perfect harmony. From a witch's point of viewpoint, the earth as well as every living thing that exists within this world possess a soul, an energetic design. In turn, witches generally, consider all-inclusive conscious of the natural world and all the world.

LIVING IN HARMONY WITH THE EARTH

The witches praise life and in the absence of life on our planet is as you probably know could not exist. In this regard witches try to establish a dialogue between themselves and Mother Nature. In fact, they might have conversations with trees, fowls, animals, or stones. In any event and more importantly, they seek to be observant and pay attention to how they can make the appropriate demands of nature. Witches are aware that we're dependent upon the earth in this regard, and it is a good idea to take part in rehearsals that benefit both us and our planet. "Its sacrosanct ground we stroll upon with each progression we take," some witches perform. They seek to live in harmony with all of nature and balance the energies which have become erratic within our modern-day, technology-driven society.

It is commonplace to refer to our world as Mother Earth as if it is actually the mother of all. That is what makes everyone and everything in the world a piece of an enormous and remote family. As you recognize that you're part of a larger, more significant whole, it becomes to becoming increasingly difficult to operate against this whole. It is detrimental to your friends, family members as well as your self. Witches try to be gentle and to be mindful of all living things as sacred, and to honor the sacredness of all things. We should try to walk with a gentle heart in a manner that is gentle, and mindful of the whole life and respect the holy nature of everything and with one another. If we are able to achieve this, then we will recover the earth, and the earth will repair us.

Green witches explicitly commit themselves to this manner Some witches might take action to protect endangered areas and wild animals, claiming that losing this potential wrongdoing is a loss to Gaia (one title for the spirit of earth; also in Greek folklore, the goddess of the earth).

Some give money or even time to causes that are biological They often channel positive energy by means of rituals and spells. As time passes, you'll get more adept at doing your part to bring greater recognition of harmony, wellbeing and success within your area of the universe and in your beyond.

Signs and Omens in Nature

A stone, a flower or herb, a tree or any other creature can have a special significance to the witch, contingent upon when and where it is seen as well as what is going on within her life at that moment. In the case of it's a wild

Rose suddenly appears in the yard of her home She may take it as a good sign that there is growing love in the house. The most skilled witches will take an additional step and thank the nature for the gift she has given to dry the flowers, then transform the small fortune into a fragrant incense that encourages love. So the witch could find her self-motivated again by an uncontaminated miraculous connection to the earth and all the tiny things people often overlook in their hectic daily lives.

REGULAR MAGICK

If you're serious about becoming a witch or performing magic, then you'll need be in touch with the world that surrounds you. Nature has lots to offer and a lot of opportunities to give the person who is. Nowadays, the largest portion of us are more familiar with computers and mobile phones, office spaces and shopping malls that have been fashioned to match the elements, whereas we're able to see how the harvest is developing in the fields, hearing the sounds of flowing streams swaying over stones, or the scent of rotting leaves in the woods' back.

Go for a stroll outdoors. Be in touch with the air passing through your hair. Pay attention to the feathered animals living in the trees within your backyard. Keep an eye on the sunset. Make time to enjoy the blooms which bloom at the center for recreation during the middle of the year.

The world of the typical is normal as it could have been, apart from the fact that it's not as common that the normal world.

the same as it ever appeared to be. However, there's not as much of it as it was just a quarter century ago, and the majority of us aren't trying to get the most enjoyment from the world often enough. When you re-discover the regular cycles of your life and begin to observe how they affect the course of your personal lives. Once you are accustomed to doing this, you'll notice you're relaxed with the world surrounding you and also with your own. It is likely that you will find it difficult to alter your daily routine to the shifting seasons as our predecessors were able to do it, nor is it necessary.

Chapter 10: Great Witch, Bad Witch: Which Is Which?

Even with the horrifying image that religions have sought to give witches they have all been concerned about helping the masses and their networks. In the time we've mentioned, fear and confusion are the root of all the nonsense that people have about witches. As you get more familiar to them, you will discover that they're very similar to any other human being; they just perceive the world a bit better.

Is there "terrible" witches who utilize their knowledge and powers for personal gain or apprehension? In fact, in the same way with "awful" Christians, "awful" Muslims and the like. Witches are distinct individuals. If you shake a trees that are not literal enough the apples that are rotten could fall off. This is just human nature. The good news is that these apples are an exception, rather than the standard.

Witchcraft and Ethics

Similar to any other human being Witches are able to stand up to problems that demand that they make moral choices. In particular, should make use of magic to use a weapon regardless of whether or not it's to get revenge? Is it possible to use magic in order to obtain what you require regardless of whether it could mean you're taking someone in danger? What is your position? the line between black and white magic?

Certain witches don't be concerned about the moral consequences that a spell can have or, but rituals--what can be said is that it performs. By casting a spell you're trying to increase the odds for your or someone who is not your support, in the event that it's for an individual. The goal is to influence an event later. As a society, we perform this every day, clearly and in different ways but when a witch performs magic she puts her entire conscious and creative attention to the task.

Wiccans as well as other witches believe that magic can have an impact that is boomerang: What you perform is returned back to the person you. If you cast an act that harms someone or someone else, you'll harm yourself in the process, or draw someone else in your path who could make the damage. Thus, witches frequently follow some variation of The Golden Rule you hurt. Therefore, witches often follow some form of Golden Rule when doing spells be considerate to the people around you and be kind towards yourself.

Magicians recognize that, even though our human spirit and personality are abounding with potential, we cannot in any way, in any way, shape, or manner predict all potential outcomes of the spell. The human mind isn't all-knowing, and at times, unrealistic goals result in disastrous results. To be to the right side of caution it is recommended to end a ceremony or practice the ritual using a phrase like, "This is accomplished for the best great of all and may it hurt none." In essence, this delegates responsibility in the end to greater (and wiser) authorities who possess an understanding of the best way to achieve the best result.

Imagine a situation in which someone Significant to You is Opposed to Witchcraft?

Engaging in debate over it is an awful thing to do. There is no way to alter any of the assumptions about spells or anything else. It is best to conduct your studies at a private location. If possible, move to the other side of the issue and try to have look at the person who is acting as your instructor. What exercises would you be capable of gaining by this limitation?

Your Personal Code

Every magickal practice starting from the Druids and the Druids to Wicca to Santeria is governed by rules which guide the practitioner and limits she will not overstep, and a central arrangement of beliefs that are a part of everything the things she performs. The central beliefs that define an individual's practice in the realm of magickal. In Wicca For instance the most important principal is not to harm anyone and no one.

However, people are also able to create their individual codes. Are you sure that yours is ascribed?

According to recent research, the culture-specific differences can affect the shaping of an individual's beliefs. In any situation, each of us has to refine our personal codes of conduct in the years we go from being children to adults. The ideals that are right for a particular person is likely to not work to another. The underlying principle of every conviction-based system is a set of rules that governs your daily life. It may be in no way connected with the opinions of others about what is good and bad.

The way you live your life can be always significant when you build your magical abilities and become more and more adept in utilizing your power. Every witch relies upon her inner voice (or the still voice, or that you can call it) when deciding on the best way to use the power of magick. There's no easy answer as to who is an excellent or terrible witch.

For those who are new to the vast world of Witchcraft You will learn the latest techniques and experiences, as well as experience emotions and new experiences while you explore your new-found way. There are some that will be shocking and some may be a challenge while others will enthralle and inspire you. The one thing that you should be certain of once you've started the journey you'll never see an identical person again.

A CONCISE HISTORY OF WITCHCRAFT IN THE WEST

They have a rich and varied cultural heritage that they continue to praise in the present. Although the origins of Witchcraft were buried in the past, they are still present today. time, it is likely that people all over the globe have been drilled with spells and Witchcraft within some kind of structure from the beginning of time. Anthropologists believe that Stonehenge might have been the sacred site at which magick ceremonies were carried out hundreds of years ago. The highly acclaimed paintings on the Trois Freres cavern wall dividers of Montesquieu-Avantes France that date over 15,000 years back, could be a result of Paleolithic communities to practice a form of magick. By painting these images people who lived in caverns searched for guidance from spirit animals to help them succeed on the hunt.

Modern witches are returning interest in the Craft. When you sign up to their groups and become a part of the new generation of magicians taking an innovative spin to an old-fashioned view. Isn't that energizing?

THE OLD RELIGION

Magick and Witchcraft both go hand-in-hand however, there are many different types of magick that fall within the broad category of Witchcraft All witches engage in magical practices in one way or the other. In the early days of humankind it was when the first people came to know. At long last, the witch-agitation diminished. It is possible that people became tired of the violence. In England it was believed that the pursuits decreased in the early 1800s. The witch resolution was eventually ended. The final execution recorded took place in Germany in 1775.

WITCHCRAFT IN THE NEW WORLD

Within the New World the practice of witchcraft developed in a complex interwoven system of beliefs and rehearsals. An array of thoughts traditions, customs, and cultures was able to coexist with some interfering with and impacting one another. Every new group of workers brought with them different perspectives and beliefs. Over period of time, they created an enthralling assemblage of magical thinking.

People who prescribe medicines from local clans of North, Central, and South. America were involved in various forms of shamanism, witchcraft and magic throughout the centuries. They used the realm of plants to heal themselves and discern the future. They contacted spirit guides, prehistoric creatures, and non-physical beings in search of a great source of guidance for crop development as well as chasing. As witches of other nations the indigenous people considered Mother Earth and every one of her creatures. As magicians across the world their world, they utilized nature's powers to produce outcomes.

In the time when European pioneers migrated to their new home in the New World, they brought their traditions along. The early pioneers were not Christians. Some adhered to an Old Religion and looked for the opportunity to test their ideas in a different place. It is believed that a significant portion of those who were part of the group were part of Indian clans, whose beliefs coincided in line with their personal beliefs.

The slave trade brought the customs that were carried by African witches and their ancestors to Americas.

Voudou devotees (voodoo), Santeria, macumba as well as other religions carried their beliefs and customs along with them across the Caribbean and to the Southern conditions in the U.S., where they remain flourishing to this day.

Witchcraft in Salem

If William Griggs, the town specialist for province Salem Village (presently Salem), Massachusetts, couldn't recuperate the poor little girl who was daughter of the Reverend Samuel Parris Griggs made sure the ladies were in awe. In this way, he initiated the notorious Salem witch hunt, which is still one of the greatest American catastrophes. Scandalous Salem witch hunt, which is one of the most infamous American tragedies.

In the beginning, young women who lived in Salem and the surrounding networks began "shouting out" the names of "witches" who had as the public can tell been the cause of their illnesses.

Between June and October 1692, 19 people were executed and another died due to witchcraft-related crimes. The experts tossed over 150 unfortunate victims into prison, and a handful were thrown in the mud, because they were allegedly allied to the criminal.

The political and religious components combined to create the witch-blight in Salem.

The ongoing epidemic of smallpox as well as threats from Indian clans has made the Indian network extremely fearful. Rivalries between competitors Rev. James Bayley of neighboring .Salem Town (presently Danvers) and Rev. Parris increased the pressure since both priests benefited from their Puritan community members' fear of Satan in order to boost their claims fame.

The insane also empowered local experts to rid the neighborhood of nonconformists and nuisances. Finances, too played a role to be considered by Salem's "witches"-- those who were sentenced received their benefits re-allocated and their properties were put into the town's fund. Certain of the executed and decried women owned property, and weren't being represented by husbands or male relatives, who didn't fit in with the male-dominated society of the day. The idea of putting these women on their own could be a part of the underlying thought process for the Salem witch trial preliminaries.

The day is today, Salem celebrates the casualties of the Salem Witch Trials with engraved stones placed in a tiny in a tree-contained park off Derby Street, close the city's waterfront as well as the visitor's area. You can take a stroll around the memorial and remember the city's break point.

Daydreaming Witches

One theory is that people who were afflicted by witchcraft during Salem actually "high" on a growth thought to be ergot, which develops in Rye bread. The psychedelic compound LSD was initially identified through Ergot. This way the strange behavior displayed by those "people in question" was likely due to the consumption of this hallucinogenic drug, and not due to the satanic affiliation.

WITCHCRAFT'S REBIRTH

Through centuries of oppression, the practice of witchcraft has never went away. It was just a matter of going underground. Witches would continue to impart the lessons of mother to girl, from father to child in secret. By way of oral traditions code, rituals, and even images, the magickal information were passed down from generation to generation in every level of the society.

Some parts of the globe, evidently did not experience the mania of witches that swept Europe as well as Salem, Massachusetts. However, the places where an atmosphere of the rage of mistreatment once erupted in witchcraft and magick, it was not the same throughout the 19th and 20th centuries.

Magick in the Victorian Era

Awe for the magickal, spiritualism, mystical quality as well as the occult, when everything is completed grew towards the end of the 19th century, perhaps in response to the age of reason's emphasis on science and rationality. The magicians of that were influential on the evolution of modern witchcraft as well as magick.

One notable person of that of the time is Charles Godfrey Leland, a Pennsylvania writer and researcher who wrote extensively about the ancient stories from various Cultures. The most acclaimed of his works, Aradia, or the Gospel of the Witches turned into a major material that helped advance the development of Neopaganism and witchcraft in the present. The other of the authors was Madame Helena Blavatsky, a native of Russia, a medium and occultist who emigrated in New York and established the Theosophical Society with Henry Steel

Alcott. Theosophy, meaning "divine shrewdness," joins ideas that originate from the Greek riddle schools, Gnostics, Hindus, and others. It was the largest magical apprehension to come out of the West in the Victorian period. The three men mentioned above were Freemasons and members of The Rosicrucian Society, which impacted their views and beliefs. The enlightening instruction of the request drew on the beliefs and customs of different cultures, as well as melded with a mind-boggling set of rituals of magical rites of the state (increasingly on this subject as outlined in The Poetry of Ritual

The Golden Dawn's magical rituals were developed by the famous British spiritualist and writer William Head servant Yeats, who was among the prominent individuals who wrote about the requests working in conjunction together with the father of the founding S.L. Macgregor Mather's.

One of the most notorious individuals of the time of the Golden Dawn was A leister Crowley who was a shady and attractive figure that has been credited with being the greatest magician of the 20th century. Following his break from the Golden Dawn, he shaped his own mysterious society known as Argentum A strum, or Silver Star as it was eventually became the chief of the Ordo Templi Orient is (Order of the Templars from the The Orient, (also known as OTO).

The majority of his work was centered around the use of sexual energy that surprised the skeptical, tense Victorians. Crowley was the writer of a variety of works on magick and occultism, Crowley additionally made one of the most popular Tarot decks, which he created along with

Lady Frieda Harris. It is called The Thoth deck.

NEOPAGANISM

Pagan was originally a derogatory phrase used by the Church to refer to people typically from the country, who were not converted to Christianity. The majority of the time today, Neopagans could be described as people that adhere to a earth-loving philosophy and strive to be within the midst of all living things in the world, just as the universe. The majority of agnostics are multitheistic. That is, they believe in a variety of gods rather than a single god or goddess. However, certain pagans might not believe in a particular higher being.

There are many different people groups. Pagan and Wiccan peoples group covers many areas and provide a variety of opinions, beliefs as well as practices. Some

Pagans are not witches or Wiccans although Wiccans as well as witches are usually thought of as being pagans. Due to the similarity between the two, they frequently connect their resources to support political, philanthropic as well as ecological and educational objectives.

MORDERN WITCHCRAFT

Over the past few decades that have passed, witches' roles have risen rapidly. It's not easy to figure out the number of people who are practicing witchcraft, a specific research conducted in 2001 by the City University of New York identified 134,000 self-described Wiccans within the United States. It's no doubt that the number has grown from then onwards.

The American Academy of Religions presently has boards to commemorate Wicca as well as witchcraft. It is believed that the U.S. Protection Department perceives Wicca as a religious authority and allows Wiccan officials to display their beliefs on canine names. According to 2006 figures there were estimated to be 1 800 Wiccans served within the U.S. military. In no doubt, the Internet is awash with information on Wiccans and the Craft.

In allowing witches around the globe to interact with one another with a non-spy and secure manner and in a secure, undiscovered way, the Internet has extended the influence of witchcraft to every corner of the world. You can now find many websites and blogs places that focus on the topics of Paganism, Wicca, witchcraft as well as magick. There are also plenty of insightful and exciting ideas and awards.

It's not a fixed conviction or rigid collection of rituals and rules The substance is a living one which is constantly evolving and growing. When instruction dispels fear and uninformed judgments, magical beliefs and practices will gain greater recognition by people of all ages and affect the spiritual evolution of everyone, with not much attention to their particular religions.

THE MAGICKAL UNIVERSE IN WHICH WE LIVE

We are in a fantastical world. Children often grasp this fact regardless of the fact that adults do. For a child it's like the world is full of possibilities for possibilities. A majority of people miss the amazing reality because they've been taught to explore the real world, and focus on the mundane aspects that make up everyday life. Magick regardless will teach you that the universe we perceive is just one of many icebergs. Once you've mastered your magical abilities and abilities, you'll discover the amazing powers that remain within the universe.

Maybe, within the most deep apprehensions that your brain has, you can find vague memories of a bygone period when you were in constant contact with planet, the universe as well as your natural instincts. In the process of strengthening your relationship with the natural world and universe and the universe, you might trigger memories. Perhaps you'll realize the fact that you are a witch in the core of your being, and have always been.

There are a variety of ways that can help you tap into your divine control as well as countless methods to harness the power of creativity from the universe. This book offers a variety of ways to think, strategies and techniques. Certain people won't speak to you, while others do.

Pick what you prefer and let the rest go. No matter what path you choose to take, once you are a witch and practice magick, you come to a pact to the universe that, when you fulfill your obligation and do your part, then the rest will unfold and the universe will also realize that when you fulfill your obligation and do your part, then the rest will unfold.

The Cosmic Web

According to scientific perspective, all energy is. The world of magic is wrapped around a vibrant web that connects everything with everything else. The grid, also known as the "astronomical web," wrap the earth in a huge bubble. It also covers everything which is here, and extends across the entire solar system as well as past. The internet is awash with simple resonances that mystics, magicians as well as other sensitive people are able to be able to feel. No matter if you're conscious of these frequencies, you're influenced by them, as well as the vibrations of your personal energy continuously influence the internet.

Energy, Energy Everywhere

Every single thing on earth emits the energy of the universe or a similarity to it. Every object has its own energies, resonances which are also called "marks." The resonances link to one another in the form of a series of confusion lines across the globe much like a huge insect-catching network. They also connect the physical and nonphysical worlds. These powerful connections allow wizards and witches to accomplish amazing things, even in the span of a lengthy distance. When you send a thought, or emotion along the energy lines to anywhere or anyone you want to connect with. It's faster than writing a book.

Consider this for a moment: what do you remember the number of times that you've received a phone call from someone that you had been pondering? This isn't an accident. The thoughts of you and another individuals are connected in the endless web even before you ever addressed one another in the physical world. When you perform the magic, you decide to connect to this infinite web. It is possible to pull some of some of these lines. First, you need to become more sensitive to these vibrations. You will also become conscious of the energetic field surrounding your.

Chapter 11: Detecting Energy Currents

Do these easy exercises to get more aware of your own energy as well as the energy in the world. If you're interested doing these things with your partner.

1. Close your eyes and place your palms in front of you. They should be facing each other at a distance of about a foot at most, a foot or. Slowly bring your palms closer to each other, but don't allow them to meet. Do you sense the energy flowing through your fingers? There could be a feeling of warmth or coldness, different levels of shivering, or even something distinct. It is possible to detect sensation or a shade. Feelings become more rooted in the event that your hands get closer to each other?

2. Choose an object, preferring something that has a distinct appearance such as plants or stones. You can run your hands through the object without touching it with your hands, trying to sense the power

that it emits. Do you feel anything? Are you able to sense warmth, coldness, or a different feeling that comes from reading the article? Are you able to get any thoughts or thoughts? Don't restrict them regardless of how they may appear unusual.

3. Ask a friend to do this exercise together. You should lie down with your eyes closed as your companion sits in front of you. Slowly, you'll see your friend push her hands towards your head and never touches your head. When you feel the power of the hand, tell her at least. Then switch sides and try the exercise repeatedly. Note what you have encountered as to be the "grimoire" or "book of shadows," an account of your magical spells as well as encounters. The notes you make will be helpful when you continue to work using different energies and also as you become more conscious of

how your individual energies change according to your mental state as well as your health and your current conditions.

THE COSMIC INFORMATION REPOSITORY

Similar to like the Worldwide Web, the grandiose web is filled with data. Every thought, word actions, feelings, and thoughts going from the beginning of time are stored on the flaming grid. Anyone who knows that password has access to this vast repository of data. Perhaps you've heard of the mystic Edgar Cayce, now and often referred to as"the "Resting Prophet." While he didn't have any formal training or medical preparation, Cayce could go into an euphoria and discover solutions for thousands of burned out people who sought his help. What did he have to do? He mysteriously "downloaded" astuteness that incredible people prior to him have "blogged" into the enormous web.

The clairvoyants aren't the only ones who gain access into information in this manner. Thousands of people are able to do it. It's just that they don't know how. Performers, artists, and designers as well as other creative individuals frequently promise information without actually having a clue about where they come from.

Mozart did not design, plan his works, or even dissect them. He just listened to the sound playing in his brain and then took a note of the music. Van Gogh declared, "I dream of painting, and then I paint my fantasy." Scientists, too are reporting discoveries that result in new discoveries in medicine, innovation as well as other areas. Everyone connects to the huge internet and gaining information from it.

Think to Quiet Your Mind

Additionally, you could benefit from the vast database of information. Being able to tap into the secrets of the past can be a great source for witches. What would it be like to have the legendary wizard Merlin leading you when you've done your magical acts?

At first it's important determine how you can relax your mind. Most of us are afflicted with minds that run like a hamster on a treadmill. When it comes to the realm of magic this is very counterproductive. There's no way to "hear" the bosses' advice if you're considering hundreds of various items. One of the best ways to express the inner nastiness is to think. If you've never considered it on your thoughts, you might think that you must sit in a lotsus posture and repeat "Oooommm" for quite a lengthy period of time. False. There is a way to go for an outdoor stroll, tune to a soothing tune (without lyrics) or watch the evening fall or weed the garden. You can also tidy up, or even put on a layer of clothing. It is important to focus all of your attention on everything you're working on, and not having interruptions that interfere.

The practice of contemplation helps you clear all the debris from your brain and to focus your thought. Additionally, it opens up the pathways for communication between you and the rest of the universe. Because the brain is the source of power of magic and mystical powers, it follows that the greater authority you have over your thinking The more effective your spells are likely to become.

Trust Your Intuition

No matter if you refer to it ESP or a feeling an instinct, gut feeling or an inner knowing or clairvoyant energy, everyone can feel an instinct. The feeling could cause hairs to grow in the back part of your neck. It could create an irritation within your solar plexus, or cause you to feel confused. The 6th sense could be able to speak to your in snaps of crisis or calm, for instance in the midst of a congestion or when you're in the process of cleaning. However, regardless of how your gut instinct communicates to you, it's crucial to remember that your alleged sixth sense is important and commonplace as the other five senses.

Consider the money you'd give on if you fell not feeling seeing, hearing and smell or even contact. Your world would become an even more unforgiving place. Try to imagine how much more you can be able to do if you had more senses on top of the five. Fortunately, you do!

Because instinct does not "bode well" (that is that it isn't based on the five faculties of our physical body) it is possible that people typically denounce its credibility. But many renowned researchers recognize that intuition has a major influence on their research. When he was in his final years, Nobel laureate Jonas Salk who discovered the immunization against polio wrote a book on intuition entitled Anatomy of Reality. The book suggested the development of imagination through the interaction of capability and the ability to think. Bill Gates stated, "Regularly you need to depend on instinct." Albert Einstein accepted "the main genuine important thing is instinct."

Intuition is the connection between your consciousness personal characteristics and the huge web. The ability to discern is the witch's most trusted partner. In certain instances, the capability is the primary aspect of spell-working. You are able to recall the qualities of different gemstones, plants or colors. Then, you can follow the recommended steps of an ritual. However, if you're not able to trust your intuition to guide yourself, you'll never achieve the capacity you're capable of. Connect with your intuition:

Listen to the "voice inside."

Concentrate on your the hunches.

Concentrate on your dreams and the things they're trying to tell you.

Notice "fortuitous events."

Keep track of the impressions, memories and pieces of information are gathered, no matter how unlikely they are in the moment, they could be interpreted as something else later on.

Once you are able to concentrate on your inner voice you will notice it become more solid and begin to channel more important data your way. The ability to rely on your intuition is a great way to improve your lives and enhance your magic ability in countless ways.

THE MOON AND YOU

One of the biggest relationships we've with the universe which we reside--and the clearest is Earth's close friend Moon. You can clearly discern the effects the moon's influence on the planet as well as Vand's inhabitants. In particular, the Moon's cycle of 28 days has an impact on the Seas the tides. However, more high tides generally are observed when the moon is full. The moon also affects the growth of crops, the climate as well as animal and fertility of humans, which is what according to the Farmers' Almanac has been claiming for over two centuries. It also affects our mood and actions. There are more babies born into the world at the time of the full moon than various times of the month. Talk to police officers or emergency room laborers about the moon's fullness and they'll tell that they encounter more emergency situations in the form of more violations, larger movements in general when the moon is at its full. It's true that the moon's fullness won't turn you into a werewolf. but it could unleash the wild side of you.

Crystal gazers interact with the moon by combining feeling intuition, sensitivity, and creativity -- the exact things witches rely upon when performing magick. This way should you want your spells to become stronger and more strong, concentrate on the moon's phases and work out ways to tap into the lunar energies.

Connecting with the Moon

Since ancient times the moon has fascinated people from all walks of life. Specialists, artists, performers and lovers, crystal gazers and magicians are all captivated by moon's captivating subject matter to study and inspire.

"Proof of Moon revere is found in such broadly shifted cultures as those of the Anasazi Indians of New Mexico, the Greeks, Romans, Chinese, pre-Columbian Peruvians, Burmese, Phoenicians, and Egyptians. In the Art, when we allude to the incredible god by the Hebrew names El or Elohim, we get terms that entered Hebrew from Arabic, where the god name 'Ilah' gets from a word that signifies 'moon.'"

www.ingramcontent.com/pod-product-compliance
Lightning Source LLC
Chambersburg PA
CBHW071448080526
44587CB00014B/2033